# Tell You What

# Tell You What
## Great New Zealand Nonfiction 2015

Edited by Jolisa Gracewood
& Susanna Andrew

AUCKLAND
UNIVERSITY
PRESS

First published 2014

Auckland University Press
University of Auckland
Private Bag 92019
Auckland 1142
New Zealand
www.press.auckland.ac.nz

Texts © the contributors
Selection and introduction © Jolisa Gracewood & Susanna Andrew, 2014

ISBN 978 1 86940 824 4

Publication is assisted by creative*nz*
ARTS COUNCIL OF NEW ZEALAND TOI AOTEAROA

A catalogue record for this book is available from the National Library
of New Zealand

Cover design: Philip Kelly Studio

Printed in China through Asia Pacific Offset Ltd

# Contents

# Introduction

'Tell you what,' someone says, on impulse or on reflection – and we're hooked. The words promise a revelation, a shift, a new truth. This book celebrates that call and response by gathering some great nonfiction reads from the last few years: a buzz of voices that captures what we were thinking.

We're surrounded by true stories these days. Reportage, memoirs, essays, musings, blog posts, tweets; so much to read, from so many places, so little time. But whether published on paper or online, or delivered aloud to a one-off audience, much of this material remains ephemeral. It holds you in its spell for a moment, then disappears into the recycling pile or browser cache.

So we've summoned a timely selection of these fugitive pieces back into the light, to reveal the strength and variety of nonfiction in New Zealand right now. Together on the page, these writers illuminate a moment in time.

*

Our inspiration was twofold. First, it had never been done before. Why, we found ourselves wondering, doesn't New Zealand have its own equivalent of the *Best American Essays* or *Best Australian Essays* series? Surely we have enough great nonfiction to fill a book on a regular basis?

Secondly, we love a challenge, and one was posed by *Metro* magazine editor Simon Wilson in July 2013, when in a review of a legendary exponent of long-form journalism, he asked: 'Where is our Janet Malcolm?' His best guess: whoever she was, she was too busy tweeting.

The response – at least, as soon as the review was posted on the magazine's website – was swift. 'It's easy to lament what we do not have in New Zealand,' responded poet and essayist (and regular tweeter) Ashleigh Young on her blog. 'Our voices necessarily come from a different place. I think we're at the beginning of something; we're witnessing a slow but sure surge of interest in the kinds of nonfiction that do illuminate things around us and *in* us.'

In fact, Wilson had it backwards, replied blogger and translator Giovanni Tiso on his own blog. 'Poetry, fiction and creative nonfiction thrive on the New Zealand web,' he argued. 'These kinds of online writing are consistently bolder, hence more relevant, than what one reads in print.' In other words, while Janet Malcolm may have a *New Yorker* budget and readership, we have broadband enough, and time. We also have an open, supportive writing community; and, while our literary marketplace is small, most editors are a friend of a friend of a friend or a retweet away.

Some of our freshest writing is definitely to be found online – fully half the contents of this collection were originally published on the web. But wherever you find it – in the unruly richness of the blogosphere, on the radio, at a live event, on a magazine rack or wrapped around your fish and chips – nonfiction is a vital part of our cultural landscape.

Steve Braunias, himself approaching the status of nonfiction national treasure, said in a speech in September 2013 that 'our most accomplished literature is our history and biography'. And yet, perhaps by virtue of its name, which tells you what it isn't, nonfiction sometimes seems to occupy a second-class status – or worries that it does. Braunias pointed to novelist Emily Perkins' blurb on the cover of his award-winning collection *Civilisation*, which praised it as being 'like a series of great New Zealand novels bound up in one extraordinary book'. His riposte: 'Will someone say on the cover of Emily's next book, "It's like a series of great books of New Zealand nonfiction bound up in one extraordinary novel"?'

Of course, these are two sides of the same coin: extraordinary novels spring from life observed – we often say they 'ring true' – while extraordinary nonfiction, as Perkins suggests, can be every bit as artful as its made-up counterpart. Undeniably, too, great books of New Zealand nonfiction hold their own as the complement to our great novels, dominating sales and doing well at awards. But whereas the short story is, as Lydia Wevers has argued, something of a national specialty, regularly anthologised and valorised by competitions, our short nonfiction still struggles to find the light. Which is why we set out to celebrate the genuine article, sufficient in itself.

Our temporal starting point for this collection was the Canterbury earthquake of September 2010, an event that shook loose our beliefs about what could happen when and where; buildings broke and words came tumbling out. Among other dates we might have chosen, this one felt somehow definitive. And then we began hunting.

Our scope was nonfiction in the broadest sense, perhaps because the word 'essay' sounds to New Zealand ears like homework; and by 'great' we meant astute, astonishing, absorbing, provocative, riveting and true. We threw a wide net, both here and overseas, for writing that told us something we didn't know, or upended something we thought we knew. We asked around for stories that had stuck with readers, that invited re-reading, that begged to be passed on.

With Emily Dickinson's line in mind – 'Tell all the truth but tell it slant' – we looked for sincerity with style. We prized distinctive voices, whether artful or blunt, exploratory or argumentative. We sought writing with a real feeling for prose; with seriousness, flourish, humour, swagger; with a sense of authority – or of gathering doubt. Writing that catches the reader by surprise is memorable; a writer taking herself by surprise is even more disarming.

We found writers pondering the cost of living, both metaphorical and literal: the trade-offs of modern life and dangerous work. We found writers on the move, tracing the travels of people, of notions, of practices and objects. We found writers pursuing the idea of home, an old theme with increasingly worldly twists. And we found 'New Zealand' all over the map: observed – and observing – from small towns, from distant metropolises and from the highest mountain in the world.

Larger-than-life figures stride through these pages, young and old: some well-known, others perfectly ordinary and yet extraordinary in their own way. There are public tragedies and private disasters; quests and questions; the odd mystery. And on every page there's an attention to the strange, slippery magic of stories – the way we pass them on or hold them close; how much of our history is hidden from view; how much of it is hiding in plain sight.

The book begins with a recollection of being shoved unexpectedly into the realm of nonfiction and ends with instructions for heading back out into the world. Along the way, you'll encounter an ICU, a credit card, a rotary clothesline, a crack in the floorboards, a builders' level, a set of bells, a hollow needle, the good knives, an open home, an egg, a window, a pair of undies, a bike helmet, a whare, a buried forest, an Elvis LP, a fish trap, a snail, a garden, a tattoo, a pair of budgies, a glittering mosaic, a uniform, an avalanche, a stethoscope, a loose weatherboard, a cold beer and an orange.

Truly, these pieces 'illuminate things in us *and* around us', making clear the connection between life and the page. If we have a lament at all, it's for all the great New Zealand non-fiction we couldn't fit within these pages. Consider this an invitation to a conversation that carries on beyond the book in your hands.

Because tell you what: there's plenty more where this came from.

*Jolisa Gracewood*
*Susanna Andrew*

# Anthony Byrt
## What I'm Reading

I'm currently staying, with my wife and seven-month-old son, at a friend's house on Auckland's west coast. We're off-grid – the power and water come straight from the sky. As a result, our days are determined as much by the weather as our boy's shifting needs. We're not completely cut off though; we have a satellite broadband connection.

Under the house's single, energy-saving lamp is a pile of books that I occasionally dig through once my son is down for the night. Some of them belong to me, but most belong to my friend: the second volume of John Richardson's Picasso biography; Colin McCahon, Elizabeth Peyton and John Currin catalogues; Svetlana Alpers and Michael Baxandall's book on Tiepolo; Daniel C. Dennett's *Consciousness Explained*; Judith Binney's *Encircled Lands*.

No fiction though. This is weird for me, because up until my son's birth, that's almost all I read. But I haven't been able to since. Most parents will probably sympathise with this; it's pretty hard to open a novel at the end of an infant-led day. But there's another factor. My son almost died in a Berlin ICU the morning after he was born. So either fiction seems a little pointless after an experience like that, or the trauma, months later, has started to take on a fictional quality: memories,

First published as a response to the 'Reading Room Questionnaire' in *Reading Room: A Journal of Art and Culture*, no. 5, *The Space of Reading* (Auckland: Auckland Art Gallery Toi o Tāmaki, 2012).

dreams and sleepy 'what ifs' have become just as untrust-worthy as each other. I haven't decided yet which one it is.

In those first weeks, the online world offered me things far more real and comforting than anything books could. I downloaded PDF reports that gave me cold statistical pos-sibilities. And I found blogs by parents in similar situations. Some had given up. Others celebrated their child's complete recovery. A few were falsely hopeful. It didn't really matter which; the important thing is that they were there, and that I'd found them.

Since leaving Berlin, my online life has become even more important. The day I booked our flights home I joined Twitter, as a way to keep in touch with the people I loved and was leaving behind. But it's grown beyond that. I'm often sur-prised by the things @AnthonyByrt says, and thrilled by what people say back to him. Their links send me places I wouldn't otherwise go, and their 140-character thoughts, when genu-inely thoughtful, twist mine too. It's a community I won't ever find between covers – a group of virtual strangers who shape how I read and survive: here, there, wherever.

# Eleanor Catton
## The Land of the Long White Cloud

There is a playful antagonism between the inhabitants of our two islands, North and South. If you're a North Islander: the South might have better views, but the North is superior because it has richer culture. If you're a South Islander: the North might have richer culture, but the South is superior because it has better views. It's a quarrel between substance and form, if you like, a question of emphasis – does a country's nature owe most to its history, or to its land? In both senses New Zealand is curiously compressed. The first Polynesian settlers landed less than a thousand years ago, the first Europeans less than three hundred. Geographically, too, the land is compact: a five-hour drive over the spine of the Southern Alps will take you through a dozen entirely different landscapes – beach river valley marshland rainforest gorge foothill highland alps plains peninsula beach – and each with its own weather, its own skies, its own quality of light. (It is a strange thing how swiftly the forecast can change in the Pacific – dress for all weather, the backcountry guides advise you, and expect four seasons in a single day.)

The South is the more visually stunning, but the North is the more populous and cultivated: this is a contrast that recalls each island's proper name. The North Island is Te Ika a Māui, 'the fish of Māui' (recounting the mythic tale of

First published in translation in *Velvet* magazine, newspaper supplement, *La Repubblica*, October 2012. Reprinted in *The Guardian*, 17 October 2013.

New Zealand's creation) where the South is Te Wai Pounamu, 'the waters of greenstone' (describing the glassy stone, prized by Māori, that is found in the swift rivers and along the savage misted beaches of the lonely south). New Zealand national identity lies somewhere between these emphases, North and South: as a bicultural nation, it must identify both as 'the place of this people' and as 'the people of this place'. The country's full name, Aotearoa, is a lovely kind of oxymoron: it translates as 'the land of the long white cloud', as if clouds were properties of the earth, or served in some strange way to invoke it.

I grew up on the South Island of New Zealand, in a city chosen and beloved by my parents for its proximity to the mountains – Christchurch is two hours distant from the worn saddle of Arthur's Pass, the mountain village that was and is my father's spiritual touchstone, his chapel and cathedral in the wild. For many years while I was growing up my parents did not own a car. We rode around town on two tandem bicycles and one single (a source of considerable embarrassment to me at the time) and at weekends we would occasionally rent a car in order to drive into the alps, and go hiking.

My father is an expatriate American; he fell in love with New Zealand in his youth and never went home. As a child I didn't really comprehend my father's affection for the land, nor for the steep-sided alp to which he returns as to an altar: Avalanche Peak, a six-hour ascent above the cloud-filled valley of the pass. My sense of injustice about our family's 'weirdness' in not owning a car was amplified by the fact that we did not own a television either – my parents were unapologetic about this, and told me very cheerfully that I would thank them for it when I was older, which was quite true. But at the time Dad's refrain 'Nature looks more beautiful in the rain' was not met with good grace. Nor was his notion that a view was something gained through effort – scenery, for him, was something that ought to be deserved.

When we reached our summit, or whatever spot was deemed by my father to be of adequately punishing distance from the car to deserve lunch, Dad would invariably find he had forgotten his Swiss Army knife (looking back, I begin to doubt he ever had one) and instead would cut cheese into slices with the edge of his credit card.

It is this kind of detail that I remember – the credit card, waxy and oiled along its edge – from our expeditions into the hills. I can recall the clean-smelling interiors of each rental car, always a different model and a slightly different shape; the empty glove box; the chipped toes of my boots; and how my hands became swollen and too weak to make a fist after a day of walking uphill. I remember, once, the rubber seal around the car door clipped into the shape of a postage stamp by alpine parrots looking for something to steal. But I don't remember the views – not as memories. In fact I am sure that I never experienced, as a child, any kind of encounter with the sublime, that catch in the throat, that tightness of the lungs, that sudden, roaring sense of one's extreme smallness in a huge, awful, beautiful world.

To experience sublime natural beauty is to confront the total inadequacy of language to describe what you see. Words cannot convey the scale of a view that is so stunning it is felt. In such moments natural beauty becomes a kind of devastation – it is pure encounter, too compressed in time and space to be properly contained. I do not feel the sublime when I look at a city, however impressive it might be in pro- portion and shadow, for the reason that a city is designed, in its substance it has been formally determined, and it has been named already by the fact of its creation. Words are adequate. I have never been moved to tears by a skyline, or a building, or a painted arch, but the sudden apparition of a peak from behind a pane of mist is enough, now, to make me cry.

I think that a child does not feel the sublime because a child need not, perhaps cannot, confront the limitations of his or her language – language, for a child, is already miraculous, supple, generous in its association, tragic, hilarious, disproportionate and huge. Looking at a cloud-filled valley was less interesting to me (or at least, no more interesting to me) than looking at my father drag his thumb along the magnetic stripe of his credit card to wipe it clean.

When I was fourteen, my father took me on a tandem bicycle trip across the mountains. He had already taken my sister and then my brother, in his turn, and as the youngest, my trip came last. We were to cross the Lewis Pass, touch the Tasman Sea, and return over Arthur's in a loop. The trip would take four days. I remember with clarity the preparations for the journey – oiling the chain, strapping down our tent, fitting the road map into the laminated pocket on the front of the bike. But I remember, too, how hopeful I was that something out of the ordinary would happen; that we would discover something, or have to endure something, out of which might come a story.

My brother had described to me an event from his own trip several years prior. He had awoken early in the morning and witnessed firsthand the birth of a calf. He and my father had pitched their tent in the stolen corner of a farmer's lot, and so it was from inside the fence that my brother saw, not 10 feet away from him, the newborn calf slither on to the grass, unfurl its legs, and stand. The story had captivated me and stirred my jealousy to such a degree that I could recall the birth almost as a memory of my own – I wanted to return there, as to a favourite page in a favourite book.

As it happened, the most memorable incident on my trip with my father was not in the least sublime. On our third day we were coasting around a downhill curve just as a three-tiered sheep truck, loaded with sheep, was climbing uphill. At the moment we passed one another, a sharp gust of wind blew up the valley and through the slats in the truck, dumping a sheet of sheep urine right over the road, and over us. My father – whose mouth had been open at the time – had shielded me completely: I was totally dry, and he was totally drenched. I didn't understand his roar of disgust and outrage until he braked violently, jumped off the bike, ran down to the creek at the side of the road, and dove headfirst into the water – by which time I was roaring with laughter. I've never forgotten it; but that owes in part to the fact that it has become a family story, part of our lore. I couldn't identify the creek, or the stretch of road, or the weather, or even the time of day.

It is curious to me how often we tend to describe the perfection and drama of the natural world, its sublime qualities, in metaphors of fakery or artificiality: 'like a postcard', 'like a painting', or latterly in New Zealand, 'like a scene from *The Lord of the Rings*'. The impulse, I think, comes from a wish to apologise for the limited capacity of the 'real' world. To grow up is to confront the disappointments of language, in a way, and to suffer the divorce between what we experience and what we imagine to be real. I was preemptively disappointed, setting out on the tandem for the mauve shadow of the hills, to know that I would in all likelihood see no newborn calves, that our adventure would have a different character to the adventure undertaken by my brother and my father. I had settled, I think, into an adult frame of mind.

I drove through Arthur's Pass recently, and stopped to climb Avalanche Peak for the first time in several years. The ascent is taxing, rising sharply through beech forest to the sudden treeline and bare grassy peaks above. The summit offers a view across the blue ranges and snow-capped summits of the island's keel. The final length of the ridgeline stands as a rocky comb of shale against the sky, dropping down on either side to wide scree slopes and rocky bluffs and nothing. Across the valley to the west is the rumple of a high glacier, a face of snow; to the east, a horseshoe cup of grey and green. And yet it is hard to describe – indescribable, until you're up there, looking down – because the mountain is something other than its substance, something more.

Travel brochures try to capture the quality of New Zealand's panoramas with adjectives – 'pristine', 'untouched', 'majestic'. But the words, however accurate they may be, seem cheap and insubstantial in the face of the real thing. The language of description is always a matter of equivalence (a word equals the thing it describes) and so cannot contend with the sublime. But the language of paradox, oxymoron and subtle contradiction – the language of children – does better. Aotearoa is a land made perfect only by its opposites, the water and the air. It is both north and south at once. It is a land that casts its shadow on the clouds.

Giovanni Tiso
# My Own Private Aotearoa

I met my New Zealander in the summer of 1991, in Edinburgh, Scotland. On my last day, we popped into the Waterstones bookshop in Princes Street and Justine bought me Keri Hulme's collection of short stories, *Te Kaihau: The Windeater*.

I read it during my long train journey back to Italy. I can still thumb through that copy and catch faint mnemonic glimpses of what it was like to not know the first thing about the country in which I now live. Although, strictly speaking, it wasn't my absolute first book by somebody I consciously recognised as a New Zealand author: earlier that year, fresh from watching Jane Campion's *An Angel at My Table*, I had read *To the Is-Land*. It has one of the great beginnings in literature:

> *In the Second Place*
> From the first place of liquid darkness, within the second place of air and light, I set down the following record with its mixture of fact and truths and memories of truths and its direction always toward the Third Place, where the starting point is myth.

That paragraph might as well have been placed at the beginning of *Te Kaihau*. These were stories that read like a novel, deeply strange and full of a terrible beauty. That was my first

First published on Giovanni's blog Bat Bean Beam, 20 August 2013 (http://bat-bean-beam.blogspot.co.nz/2013/08/my-own-private-aotearoa.html).

encounter with the unease and foreboding that mark New Zealand literature, and also with the assuredness of its voice. It was *exciting*.

\*

Nineteen ninety-one was my first year out of high school. At university, I enrolled in physics, and it took all of two weeks to figure out what an utterly preposterous decision it had been. However, I had to hang around for a while and sit one exam before transferring to another course in order to qualify for a deferral of my (compulsory) military service. The physics buildings at Milan State University included a large study room which the more senior students referred to as 'New Zealand'. I never found out why.

\*

I transferred to the faculty of Modern Letters, where, by applying myself over the next several years, I successfully failed to graduate. There they made me read Katherine Mansfield. She was easy to admire but I didn't find her as exciting. Then Justine joined me in Italy, which gave me both a reason and the means to learn about the place she came from.

In October 1994, following the success of *The Piano*, the New Zealand Film Commission took a festival to Milan entitled 'The Last Wave: The New New Zealand Cinema'. (The oldest film was *Smash Palace* and it's not as if the country had produced more than a dozen features before it, but we'll go with 'new'.) It was a very good selection. We saw *Utu*, *Ruby and Rata*, *Desperate Remedies*, *Ngati*, *Jack Be Nimble*, *Old Scores* and a series of shorts. We missed *Vigil* and *Smash Palace*. *Utu* perplexed me a little. I liked *Ngati* most of all. *Desperate Remedies*, which seemed a good romp back then, turned out to have dated rather badly when I saw it a few years later on television. Or maybe I was looking for something else from New Zealand cinema by then.

Aside from the saturating light that I remembered from *Te Kaihau*, two images in particular stayed with me from those films: the creature being pulled out of the drain in Alison Maclean's short *Kitchen Sink*; and a sequence towards the beginning of the otherwise forgettable horror *Jack Be Nimble* in which a housewife is repeatedly lashed in the face by wet clothes hanging from a rotary clothesline in the wind. The darkly humorous mystery/magic and the unthinking violence of the everyday.

*

A story in *Te Kaihau* ends with one of those outrageous questions that a writer is not supposed to ask:

> Have I told you anything?
> Has it meant anything to you?
> Or is it all just writing?
> All just words?

I realise now that in the four or five years before leaving Italy – even before there was a reason or a plan – I was building a country in my head, and that although it relied on the conversation and the personal stories of the few New Zealanders I knew (Justine, mostly), it was also, if not primarily, a literary country, a cinematic country, a country of visual arts and music.

We went to a rather unfortunate Crowded House concert. We saw *Once Were Warrior*s (in Italian). I read some more Janet Frame, and one of those collections of short stories. I failed to read Alan Duff. There was Fred Dagg. There was a wonderfully tatty Front Lawn T-shirt. Then, for Christmas of 1995 – inscriptions can be so precious, so precise – another book-gift from Justine, purchased at the only English language bookshop in town: *the bone people*.

I read it that winter, feverishly (literally, as I was in bed with the flu), and then again later that year or early the next, during the twelve months I served in domestic exile as a conscientious objector. It may well have been the last novel in which I utterly lost myself, just when I needed to. It was also bigger than the country I had built inside my head. *Much* bigger, and infinitely lonelier, and stronger. I couldn't mine it for information, as I did other things. It transported me, rather.

I wanted to follow that voice, even though the foreboding hadn't disappeared. The 'human-wounded land'.

✻

The real country differed from the imagined country in ways that I couldn't begin to recount. We arrived just in time to see state-sponsored ads on national television encouraging citizens to dob in their benefit-cheating neighbours. It was a shock even for Justine, who had left a few months into the life of the Fourth National Government, before Ruth Richardson really got into her work.

But it's more than that. My New Zealand, the country I had built in my head, was a place that cared for its pasts, and looked to the future through anxious young eyes. There were children at the heart of every story: Tione and Ropata in

*Ngati*. Rata's son, Willie. Flora McGrath. Simon/Clare. Little Janet herself. Children possessed of a laconic wisdom, often troubled, sometimes unable to speak. All around them was the history, etched like scars on the landscape. This was New Zealand before *The Lord of the Rings*, not yet the ultimate, hyper-marketed endpoint of an English colonial fantasy. I found it, even in its darkest moments, enormously sympathetic. But it's there, it's not unreal. And I still search for it.

## Lara Strongman
# A Song From Under the Floorboards

When I was seven or eight years old, my family moved into a Georgian house in a cathedral town in the southwest of England. The house was built of rendered brick and stone. It had once been quite grand, by our standards at least; it had large sash windows, tall French doors, and a servants' wing of four small rooms which jutted into the walled back garden. My upstairs bedroom had a disused fireplace and an old plumbed wash basin. It also had a crack between the wide oak floorboards where I posted letters to the future.

We lived in that house for about three years, sometime between the hot summer of 1976 and the rise to power of Thatcher's Conservatives in 1979. It was a time of rolling strikes and industrial unrest; I remember the interminable power cuts during which, unable to read, I lay in bed looking out of the window as the night closed in. I was a bookish child; I spent most of my time escaping into other worlds. For one glorious year I was a paid-up member of the Puffin Club, with a badge and a quarterly magazine about new children's books arriving in the post. We left for New Zealand during the so-called Winter of Discontent, early in 1979, when the snow lay in great drifts over the hedges in the fields. I wore my Puffin Club badge on the plane.

First published on Lara's blog Art, Life, TV, Etc., 6 March 2011 (http://cherylbernstein.blogspot.co.nz/2011/03/song-from-under-floorboards.html).

My favourite books were those which revealed the secret strangeness in the midst of the everyday. There was the extra hour struck after midnight by the clock in Philippa Pearce's *Tom's Midnight Garden*, where a modern boy opens the back door to find a sunlit garden and a girl dressed in old-fashioned clothes ready to play with him. There was Joan Aiken's *Midnight Is a Place*, where the hero Lucas falls on hard times and becomes a tosh boy, trawling the sewers under Regency London for ancient treasure in the company of a homicidal maniac. I never tired of the gentle weirdness of Tove Jansson's *Comet in Moominland*, which recounts a journey taken across the hot undersea sand on stilts after a comet passes too close and the sea dries up; E. C. Spykman describes something similar in *A Lemon and a Star*, where one day all the water in the town reservoir disappears and the children walk across the cracked mud to an island they've never seen before. Natural disasters, supernatural visitations and wrinkles in the fabric of time heralded the beginning of perilous adventures.

From my life in the world of books, I strongly suspected that real life similarly concealed secret places where the past intersects with the present and where the world of appearances is turned on its head. Like many British children of my age, I spent my childhood tapping walls in an attempt to find sliding panels and priest's holes. I peered hopefully into wardrobes. I looked for hidden drawers in old desks. I scanned pebbles on the beach in the hope of finding a moonstone. I lay on my back on the carpet and imagined the house turned upside down, with light fittings sprouting out of the floor and the chairs on the ceiling. And I lived in perpetual hope of discovering one of the Roman hoards of gold coins which were still, occasionally, being dug up in suburban gardens in the 1970s. I understood from Puffin books that time and place are not always cast in stone and that something strange could happen at any moment, and I kept a close watch on the world so that I would know when it did.

When I posted the notes through the crack in my floorboards, I imagined a girl in the future reading them. 'I am seven years old,' I wrote, 'and I live with my father and my mother and my brother and two cats. My cat is called Hoffman and he is black and one quarter Abyssinian and my brother's cat is ginger and he is called Tractor.' I wrote the kind of letter you might have written to a pen friend in the 1970s. There was a dark hidden space between the floor of my bedroom and the ceiling of the rooms below where my notes, folded into quills, piled up over a period of months. It crossed my mind after a while that the notes might stay there for a very long time, until the house was demolished or the floorboards taken up. I wrote in pencil as I thought that ink might fade, as felt-pen drawings pinned to the wall do over time. I wanted my notes to reach someone, in the future. It's the reason a writer writes.

Our house was number one in a street of semi-detached townhouses, built about 1830, at the time that the cholera epidemic swept through the city. The house pre-dated the European colonisation of New Zealand. Its stone steps were worn down in the middle by a century and a half of occupation. Our next-door neighbours through the dividing wall were an elderly couple, Bill and Jane Hoskins. Their house was the mirror image of ours, except they had deep red velvet curtains and thick carpet that your feet sank into and which made your ankles wobble. On our side there was worn sisal that gave your knees a nasty graze when you fell over and slid along it. The Hoskins' hallway had black and white tiles, like a stately home, and there were lilac trees in their garden whose heavy perfume wafted over the brick wall in spring. Jane cooked on a venerable Aga stove. There were piles of books everywhere.

The son of a local baker, Bill Hoskins was a retired professor of history from Oxford. He founded the first department of local history at a British university; his particular contribution was the impact of economic activity on the British landscape. By the time we met him he had written a dozen scholarly and popular books and had made two TV series for the BBC, the first in 1972 based on his best-selling book *The Making of the English Landscape* (1955) and the second in 1976, called *The Landscape of England*. On my tenth birthday he and Jane wrapped up a Victorian finger bowl from their collection for me. I took it out today in Christchurch, New Zealand – where it has survived a journey across the world and two major earthquakes – and held it and thought of them. When Bill died in 1992 they put up one of those circular blue historical plaques on the house where he was born.

Bill Hoskins could look at the landscape and tell you a 2000-year-old history of the people who had lived and worked and died on it. He campaigned endlessly, and successfully, to save the ancient landmarks of the city from modern development: not just the buildings, but the open spaces, such as the Bull Meadow just outside the old stone walls of the city which bounded the old Jewish cemetery. He prevented the Bull Meadow from being ploughed under by an inner-city bypass in the mid-1970s. Bill Hoskins was concerned with memory. His life was spent recalling the past to the notice of the present. He was determined that we should not forget.

'Forgetting remains the disturbing threat that lurks in the background of the phenomenology of memory and the epistemology of history,' wrote the French historian of memory,

Paul Ricoeur.* I've been thinking a lot about the danger of forgetting, in the past ten days since the Christchurch earthquake.

Quite simply, we forgot about earthquakes. We lived as if they didn't exist; we paid lip service to the idea that some day the 'big one' would strike, but I don't think we really believed that it would happen during our lifetimes. Earthquakes remained a perpetual abstraction in a world of possibility; something that had happened in the past and may happen again in the distant future but not here and now in the life of the present. Earthquakes were essentially fiction, like dried-up seas and clocks striking thirteen. I forgot the incontrovertible fact that despite ten years in earthquake-prone Wellington, the biggest quake I've ever previously experienced was in Christchurch in the mid-1980s, when the windows rattled and the light bulb swung in a crazy arc and *we had no idea what was happening.*

We forgot that it is inevitable, living in New Zealand, that one day the ground will shake and cracks in the road big enough to swallow a bus will suddenly open up and that in Christchurch water from the underground cathedral of aquifers over which this city is built will rise to the surface and choke entire suburbs in filthy silt. It had happened before, but little about the design of our central city suggested that we had remembered. We had forgotten that the spire had fallen off the cathedral twice before during major earthquakes. I'd seen those famous historical photographs of the damaged cathedral, but I realise now that I'd dismissed major earthquakes as *something that happened in colonial times.* In stories. Not now. Because it hadn't happened within living

---

* Paul Ricoeur, *Memory, History, Forgetting* (Chicago and London: University of Chicago Press, 2004), p. 412.

memory, effectively it was as if it had never happened. I think collectively we forgot that the modern world remains subject to ancient and implacable natural forces. That modernity is not a cure for nature.

Previous generations, closer to the last event, hadn't forgotten. Earlier this week it was widely reported that a crane driver found two time capsules in the rubble under the toppled statue by British sculptor Thomas Woolner of John Robert Godley, one of the founding fathers of the city. There have also been reports of another capsule in the base of the metal cross which surmounted the spire of the cathedral. The time capsules – messages from the past – are now in the care of Canterbury Museum, where they will be opened slowly and carefully by conservators in order to preserve the material fabric of the message. I am, in a way, less interested in what they have to say than in the fact that they felt they had to say it; that citizens of the past knew there would be a time when the statue would be removed from its base by forces natural or otherwise and they could speak without constraint to the future.

You can see it in the landscape. You can see it in the sharp outlines of the Port Hills at the edge of the city – which, since the earthquake, are now some two feet higher than they were last Monday week. You can see that New Zealand is a young country, whose shape is still being formed by the movement of tectonic plates. Poet James K. Baxter described it as a 'cold threshold land', whose mountains 'crouch like tigers'.* A hard place to live. When we came to New Zealand, what I missed the most – along with the built history – was the soft green Wordsworthian folds of the English hills, worn down

---

\*    James K. Baxter, 'The Mountains', 1942.

by centuries of cultivation and weather and the sheer force of history. New Zealand's landscape looked sharp and hard and brash by comparison, and its buildings looked provisional rather than solid and venerable like the house we'd left. But thirty years later, it feels like home.

When artist Rita Angus wrote in 1946 that she was 'colonial, six generations, and for me New Zealand is in essence medieval', she was presumably referring to the relatively short duration of New Zealand's European cultural history as well as to the comparative longevity of her own family's place within it.* In the late 1940s, thirty years before the Māori Renaissance informed a more critical view of its history, New Zealand felt like a young country to its Pākehā artists and writers; and with the youth came a consequent insecurity as well as an uneasy self-consciousness about its identity which has never really evaporated (although they feel very far away at the moment, the arguments around New Zealand artists' participation in the Venice Biennale are a classic case in point).

Long before the Greendale and the Port Hills earthquakes laid waste to the historical quarters of Christchurch city and its sandy and swampy suburbs, heritage buildings were being torn down to allow shoddy development in their places. We were always razing the place to the ground and starting again. We are, effectively, at a medieval stage of history. It is more critical than ever that we safely preserve the heritage we have left, and that we construct new buildings, and urban spaces, with an expansive vision worthy of future generations, a vision that allows the past a continued life in the present. Because without it, we're lost.

---

* Rita Angus, 'Rita Angus', *Year Book of the Arts in New Zealand*, no. 3, 1947, p. 68.

I'm an art historian because I know that historical art brings the past nearer – art is, like cinema, a time machine[*] – and because I believe that contemporary art has something to tell us about the present and might, at its best, reveal a new way of looking at the future. When the Minister for Earthquake Recovery, Gerry Brownlee, says that 'heritage is both forward and back' he is absolutely right. But when he says that – apart from a few civic buildings – the heritage buildings which remain 'have no place in our future history' he is demonstrably short-sighted.[†] Demolishing our history offers no useful solution to the fears of the present day. Without the material presence of the past we are cut off from our collective memory, and there is worse danger in forgetting. Like the world of speculative fiction, the everyday world is capable of sudden and violent change at any point and the more information we take forward with us from the past the better we are equipped to deal with the great and certain strangeness of the future.

---

[*]   Philip Matthews (@secondzeit), '"I think cinema itself is a time machine" – Apichatpong Weerasethakul', tweet, 5 March 2011, 8:47 a.m.
[†]   'Brownlee takes hard line on damaged heritage buildings', *New Zealand Herald*, 5 March 2011.

# David Haywood
## What Not To Expect

*At 12.51 p.m. on 22 February 2011, I had just finished writing about the arrival of my daughter, Polly, who had been born three weeks previously. A moment later, my computer exploded all over the room. That evening, sheltering in a tent in our garden with my family, I composed the following piece on my smartphone.*

### A Moment of Silence. Then a Wail of Sirens.

The first jolt knocked me off my feet. A desktop computer landed near my head and exploded into parts. Every piece of furniture was moving. A heavy wardrobe thudded onto the floor beside me. The desk upended itself; my filing cabinet toppled over and blocked the doorway. In the kitchen I could hear crockery shattering, and books tumbling from shelves in the sitting room.

I discovered the impossibility of taking useful action during a strong earthquake; the only option is simply to endure. Time slows down. After the shaking stopped, there was a moment of silence. Then a wail of ambulance sirens.

I shoved the filing cabinet out of the way, struggled to open the jammed study door, sprinted outside. White with dust, my

The first part of this piece was published on David's blog Southerly on Public Address, 22 February 2011 (http://publicaddress.net/southerly/a-moment-of-silence-then-a-wail-of-sirens/) and in the *Guardian*, 22 February 2011. The second part appeared on Southerly, 26 August 2013 (http://publicaddress.net/southerly/continuing-after-a-short-interruption/).

three-year-old son, Bob, was emerging from under the floor-boards where he had been hiding, in a bid to avoid attending kindergarten. He asked unsteadily: 'What happened, Daddy?'

The world had been transformed. A slurry of sand and water was fountaining from fissures in the road. Our lawn had been torn apart by giant 5-metre-deep cracks; one of the cracks ran right through our home – breaking it into two separate halves. The foundations beneath the rear half of the house had collapsed; the verandah hung in tatters like a broken umbrella. In the kitchen every plate, cup and dish was broken. A solitary picture remained on the walls of our hall, tilted at a crazy angle.

My wife, Jennifer, emerged from the back garden clutching our three-week-old daughter. Later we discovered a mound of fallen books in the sitting room – engulfing the crib where she usually sleeps.

We live on the banks of the Avon River. As my wife and I stood on the front lawn, uncertain of what to do next, a huge aftershock struck. Trees and telephone poles swayed like drunken men; the river gathered itself into a wave and surged across the towpath. On the opposite bank, the road suddenly collapsed beneath a car, opening up a giant sink-hole. A man crawled out of a window, checked the car, swore.

A woman was screaming nearby. On the footpath I discovered our neighbour – streams of mascara running down her cheeks. A chimney had fallen through the ceiling of the room where she was having lunch with her elderly father.

'It's my birthday today,' she sobbed, 'my house has been destroyed.' Along the street other shell-shocked neighbours were emerging.

A procession of city workers began to trickle down the footpath. Their suits and dresses were torn and dusty; the hems of their clothes wet with mud. Soon there was a continuous stream of bedraggled escapees making their way homeward on foot. Some were weeping. Others spoke to us of impassable roads, buildings destroyed, bodies lying beneath ruins.

This morning our family had a house; tonight – as with many other Christchurch families – we live in a tent. But elsewhere in the city there are those whose loved ones will never return home. As I write, the radio informs me that hundreds still lie buried in the rubble.

Thus we must count ourselves among the lucky; it could so very easily have been otherwise.

## Continuing After a Short Interruption

*By a small miracle, my computer hard drives survived that day, and a couple of years later I was able to recover the data and finally post on my blog the piece I had been writing that day just before the earthquake struck.*

Two traumatic incidents within the space of forty-eight hours is really too much.

The first incident occurred following a visit to the barber. Bob had been exceedingly – not to say unnaturally – well behaved during his haircut, and I suppose he had lots of parent-embarrassing energy that needed to be released.

As we were riding the lift to the parking building, he began to expound upon the strange feeling of suddenly having less hair: 'My neck feels like a snow-penguin, and also like a big bag of ice is weighing on my throat, and also like my head has been chopped off by scissors . . .'

Our fellow lift-traveller, an elderly lady, felt moved to inter-ject a question. 'Has Daddy taken you to the hairdressers?' she asked.

Bob broke off his monologue in mild surprise. 'No,' he said sorrowfully. 'Rats ate my hair.'

The elderly lady swivelled her head in my direction and gave me a long, condemnatory stare. Possibly the sort of accusing gaze that you inflict upon a man who lets rats eat his son's hair; possibly the look reserved for a man who raises his son to tell such outrageous lies.

Two days later and the psychological scars of this con-demnatory stare were just beginning to heal when a second traumatic incident occurred. My blissful Saturday night slumbers were interrupted by Jennifer poking me in the back with an insistent finger. 'Wake up,' she said. 'It's time.'

Oh dear, I thought, has it been nine months already?

The still-sleeping Bob was put under the supervision of a kindly neighbour. Jennifer and her surprisingly heavy suitcase were loaded into our car. We set forth through the dark night to hospital.

In the maternity ward, Jennifer unpacked her suitcase to reveal a laptop, an external hard drive, a draft doctoral thesis from one of her students, and a small quantity of baby clothing. In short order, she managed to reconfirm her dis-covery that midwives are really annoyed by maternity patients working on laptops.

I sat beside her bed in the useless manner that I'd perfected when Bob was born. Occasionally I would hand Jennifer a glass of iced water. The midwife checked progress and made pointed comments about the laptop.

After a few hours it became obvious that events were inex-orably under way. The laptop was removed from Jennifer's reluctant hands. My useless strategy of iced water was upped to an almost-as-useless strategy of hand holding and back rubbing. 'You probably want to consider some pain relief at this point,' said the midwife.

'I'm okay,' said Jennifer.

Poor Jennifer looked anything but okay. The birthing process was reaching its final stages. Her breathing came in huge, ragged gasps; her teeth were clenched with pain. It was agonising to watch. I'd have been swearing my head off, screaming for an epidural – but Jennifer just grimly worked her way towards delivering the baby.

Polly was born shortly after dawn. 'You can cry if you want to,' said the midwife, who seemed slightly disappointed by our lack of waterworks.

I held Polly while the midwife organised the weighing scales. 'I've delivered hundreds of babies,' she remarked. 'Your wife is a very strong woman, isn't she?' During the pregnancy there had been a few moments of disagreement over Jennifer's intention to stay working until the baby was born. That all seemed to be forgiven now. 'I'll make your wife some Marmite on toast,' decided the midwife.

It was extremely good Marmite on toast. I was allowed to eat a slice – even though I hadn't done anything.

Shortly thereafter Jennifer and Polly were wheeled down to the parking bay, and loaded into our car for transfer to the post-natal unit across town. I wondered, for the second time in my life, how the district health board had managed to come up with a system that requires parents to play dodgem in the streets of Christchurch with two-hour-old babies on board. For some reason, most drivers in our province become borderline psychopaths as soon as they sit behind a wheel. Indeed, even the most responsible Cantabrian motorist won't hesitate to ram your car if they think it'll shave thirty seconds off their journey.

By the end of the trip my body had never contained so much adrenaline. Perspiring with anxiety, I gingerly transferred Jennifer and Polly into a wheelchair, and delivered them carefully to the post-natal ward. 'Lift's broken,' said the receptionist. 'Wifey'll have to trot up the stairs, okay?'

'No, it's certainly not okay!' I yelped. 'She's just given birth. This is unacceptable! I've had medical advice that my wife mustn't walk. I demand that you provide a lift! Our midwife ordered me to take extra-good care of her – this is an outrage!'

'Hmm,' said the receptionist. She called a nurse. The poor nurse spent twenty minutes with us, traipsing back and forth all over the hospital, locking and unlocking doors, until eventually she discovered a route that allowed us to reach the post-natal ward via a lift. She wasn't best pleased.

'I could actually have walked up the stairs,' said Jennifer, after the nurse had gone. 'But you seemed to think that you were being helpful.'

Jennifer and Polly were assisted into bed for some much-needed sleep. Later that afternoon I took Bob along for a visit. 'We've moved your wife to a new room,' explained a helpful hospital midwife. 'I'll show you the way.' Her nurses' shoes squeaked along the shiny corridor while she engaged Bob in friendly conversation:

'And do you have a new sister or a new brother?'

'I have a new sister,' said Bob, 'and when she's older I'm going to buy her a gun. And I'll have a gun too, and I'm going to weld sockets on our guns so that I can tow them with my truck. Then we're going to shoot kiwis, and their meat will fly through the air, and land in a basket. And a robot will cut the meat into slices so that we can take it home to eat. I've already designed the robot.'

Jennifer was tucked up in bed wearing a nice white hospital nightgown. Her long hair was fanned across the pillows. She held a tiny bundle in her arms.

'Hello Mummy,' said Bob, putting his head on one side to get a better view of his new sister.

'Hello Bob, it's very nice to see you,' said Jennifer. 'Would you like to sit here and hold Polly?'

'Why is she so tiny?' asked Bob indignantly, with the air of a man who's been handed an insufficiently large portion at a restaurant.

I had a sudden recollection of Bob attached to a tangle of tubes in the intensive care unit. 'You were *much* smaller than Polly when you were born,' I said.

'She's been breast-feeding really well,' Jennifer told me. 'Apparently we can go home tomorrow.'

The next day Bob made a large placard for our front door: 'Welcome Home Polly!' He was almost dancing with excitement as he introduced his new sister to our house. 'This is the hall, Polly. This is the sitting room. This is my bedroom. Here's where you're going to sleep, Polly. Can you see the river? When you're older I'll build a boat and take you rowing there.'

'Please read us *Mike Mulligan and His Steam Shovel*,' he announced. 'I'm sure Polly would really like that.' Bob retrieved the book from the shelf and thrust it into my hands.

'Perhaps you could look after the children while I get unpacked,' said Jennifer, handing my daughter to me.

Polly snuffled into my neck as I manoeuvred myself carefully onto a chair. Bob plonked himself heavily into my lap.

Our offspring were in the plural now, I thought. One child is the sort of accident that could happen to anyone – it doesn't really conclusively prove that you're a parent. But having two children is the final nail in the coffin of parenthood. There's no escaping it now.

Bob and Polly snuggled warmly against me. I read aloud the words, 'Mike Mulligan had a steam shovel, a beautiful red steam shovel. Her name was Mary Anne.' And I thought: being a parent isn't *such* a bad thing, is it.


## Aftermath

In the aftermath of the earthquake, my entire neighbourhood was condemned – our futures were rewritten; all our plans undone. To claim our insurance policy, I was forced to disassemble our house, and then to reassemble it in the rural Canterbury town of Dunsandel.

My reluctant career as a builder has meant that I haven't been able to spend time with Polly as I once did with Bob. There have been no gentle bike rides beside the river. Polly's life has been packed full of building, plumbing, electrical work. She knows the difference between a Scrulox and a Pozidriv screw; she can trot off to the workshop and bring back the builders' level or the electric plane.

While others suffered so much more, this is, I suppose, my greatest personal loss from the earthquakes and the bureaucratic disaster that has followed. Eighteen months of seven-day weeks and long working days putting a house together again is a lot of missed time in the life of a two-year-old, and there's no way of getting it back. I hope that Polly won't feel the weight of these lost years, but I will always regret them.

# Nic Low
## Ear to the Ground

Christchurch. I grew up in Christchurch. It was a quiet, peaceful place. At the age of twenty, I'd finish work round midnight, drop my skateboard to the cobbles and clatter home. My wheels were often the loudest sound. I'd roll down Colombo Street, past the straggle of hoodie kids awaiting the last bus, then cut through the bleak granite expanse of Cathedral Square. I could hear street-sweeper trucks, and the murmur of the last-drinks crowd at Warner's, and something else too, just on the edge of my hearing. From the eastern corner of the square rose a shrill electronic whine. It was like having a mosquito trapped inside your skull. It was maddening.

The sound was produced by a device attached to the offices of the local newspaper. People over the age of twenty-five couldn't hear it. Only young people could hear it. It was designed to stop us loitering and drive us away. And it wasn't just *The Press* broadcasting that needling drone. It felt like the whole city. The sound was the suburban status quo running smoothly in its tracks, and the tiny wheels of petty bureaucracies, and the antique machinery of monocultural privilege. Once you hit your late twenties and began thinking respectable thoughts, you'd gain immunity. But it was getting to everyone I grew up with. Change felt impossible. The rest

First published in longer form in *Griffith Review 35: Surviving*, January 2012 (https://griffithreview.com/articles/ear-to-the-ground/). A version also appeared in *The Press*, 23 February 2012.

of the country thought us stiff and stuck-up and white. The vibrant subcultures that grew in the cracks felt under permanent siege. No matter how we'd enjoyed childhood, no matter the family ties and lovers and landscapes, that sound drove us to leave.

I moved to France, then Australia. I remained proudly Kiwi, yet at odds with the city that formed me. Each time I returned to see family and friends, Christchurch felt a little more empty. There were flashes of colour, but the stern stone façades and endless one-way streets dominated. People and energy seemed to drain away like so much rain from the city's slate roofs. On one visit I published an overheated opinion piece in *The Press* about the city's out-of-sight, out-of-mind approach to youth and change. I was politely told to piss off back to Australia. It seems the feeling was mutual.

Then, early on a cold spring morning in September 2010, I was holidaying with my parents in Tasmania. We stopped at a church fair. A man sold us a jar of honey. He asked where our accent was from.

Christchurch, he repeated, looking concerned. Is your house okay?

The question made no sense. Everything was always okay in Christchurch.

And so, a radical thing has happened to a conservative place. I have returned after each quake, full of love and trepidation, like visiting an estranged family member on their deathbed. I can no longer hear that whining sound coming from the square. Partly because I am a bit older, and I can see that plenty of the whining was my own restless impatience. But mostly because it has been drowned out by something much deeper, something much older. It is the sound of the earth, and the feelings the earth awakens in people. It is partly fear and it is partly strength. I am trying to understand the ruined city's new resonance.

*

When the first quake struck, the heavy bronze bells in the cathedral swayed and rang a ghostly warning across the city. My younger brother woke to the jolt and his first thought was *Shit, that must have been Wellington, and it must have been catastrophic.*

Luckily, it was neither. The bricks and concrete and glass fell into empty streets. It was the first time in modern history a 7-plus quake had hit an urban centre with no deaths. The quake was an ocean swell, a great rolling wave that rose and fell but left things much as they were. It scared the hell out of people, and houses cracked and the ground flooded with a fine mud, but it did not truly destroy the city's sense of safety. We had building codes, by god. Building codes and insurance. We had our deeply ingrained sense of luck. Even our earthquakes fit the pattern.

When I visited in December 2010, the main evidence of the quake was a rash of blue tarps over the city's roofs. Piles of fallen chimney bricks lined the streets like little altars. There were a few cleared sites and some older buildings were fenced off. Everyone I met was compelled to share their stories, and those of their neighbours, all of whom they now knew. It was as if the quake had been a synchronising of watches, a zeroing of disparate lives that gave everyone a common origin: *We survived the quake. We were scared shitless, and it's been a drag boiling the drinking water, but we all survived.* The gratitude was palpable. It felt like the city was a bit more willing to smile, even if its front teeth had been knocked out.

By the time I boarded a plane for Melbourne, the narrative was clear. You have a crisis, you respond, things get fixed up and life returns to normal. *The Press* published a letter to the editor claiming damage to the red-light district was a warning from God. Those little wheels began to turn. Things were going to be okay.

*

Somewhere down by the hospital, in the crook of the river, is the site of a disaster, perhaps the area's first. The place was called Puari Pā. Our Waitaha and Ngāi Tahu ancestors lived here, moving through the landscape on foot, to the swamps and marshes, the grasslands and forests beside the river, hunting and gathering food, listening for the whoop of kererū. They used the long, hollow bones of bird wings as kōauau flutes, and made pūtōrino trumpets from hardwood. Visitors were welcomed with the high and lonely cry of the karanga, and challenged with haka. The language itself that filled the landscape is deep and round. To my ear, the word for 'world' sums this up: ao.

European whalers came in the 1830s, and European interest in settlement grew throughout the 1840s. For the people at Puari and the other Ngāi Tahu settlements, here was the first great rupture, the break point between one society and the next. It was a slow-motion disaster; it was catastrophic, and it was not. It was the founding of the city – land for my first European ancestor, William Newnham, in 1850. It meant the ring of picks on rock as foundation stones went down, and the nasal stammering of Māori spoken with a common cold; the sound of corks worked out of bottles, fence posts hammered in, the sudden thunder of horses and guns. Demand for land was fierce. Kemp's Deed was inked in 1848 by the chiefs of Ngāi Tahu and the land passed over. Ten per cent was to be held aside for the tribe, written into the deed of sale. The land was not held aside. The land was cleared and planted with oaks and willows. Christchurch would be an idyllic, pre-Industrial Revolution English town.

Ngāi Tahu were moved out to reserves. When visiting they camped near Puari at Little Hagley Park, squatters on their own land. The sound of their presence in the landscape was silenced, and this silence became the true marker of the disaster. Children were forbidden to speak Māori at school; the later Tohunga Suppression Act attempted to stop priests from practising their chants and prayers. Ngāi Tahu presence in the city was reduced to the cry of a produce seller in Market Square.

In Christchurch, perhaps more than any other sizeable New Zealand city, there has been almost no visible Māori presence. But even if a disaster is not named, or addressed, it doesn't go away. The damage of that forced displacement was felt through the whole of society. The tribe did not stop fighting for redress for one day. And the geography of the ancestors – the pā and kāinga sites, the trails, the swamps, rivers and marshes – was still there, just beneath the surface.

*

The sound arrived first.

John Dodgson is an organist. To his trained ear it was the blast of a low C, the deepest note on the scale, coming from everywhere at once. He knew instantly what it was. My father, a jazz musician, knew it too. The sound came, and the fear came, and it surged up from a sound and a feeling into a

mighty weight that roared through the house like an invisible freight train, twisting and popping the joists and beams,
bursting open walls and floors. The ground tore itself up by
the roots, and with sudden and extreme violence shrugged the
people off.

The roar is louder than anything we can imagine. It's the
sound of a tectonic plate moving, and buildings collapsing and
books and furniture going over, and it rises up through the scale
to the wild crash of every fork and glass and plate hurled from
every cupboard in your house, in every house, in every street.
It's the sound of *the ground beneath your feet*, and *bedrock*
and *safe as houses* being torn down. It's the death of the city's
narrative. Imagine the noise of it. Imagine the fear.

If the September earthquake was a wave, the February
one was a sledgehammer. It was only 6.3 in magnitude but
the g-force, the sudden ground acceleration, was among
the highest ever recorded. From the quake's heart in Banks
Peninsula the ground jolted violently towards the city then, as
the crust of the earth rose, then fell, a second massive shock
rose up to meet it. The two shockwaves collided. This time the
impact was catastrophic.

The cathedral spire and its enormous bells were thrown into
the square. All across the city old brick buildings exploded.
The central city's Victorian façades were tossed directly onto
people and cars below. Buildings corkscrewed on their foundations and buckled and fell, and great halos of dust rose in
their place. The Pyne Gould Guinness office tower came down
one floor at a time. Those on the top rode it down like a great
concrete wave. Those beneath were crushed. In the Durham
Street Methodist Church three people were killed while dis-
mantling the huge pipe organ. I can only imagine the noise
when the roof caved in.

As the buildings came down, the swamps and marshes and ancient, buried waterways rose up. From the sewers, from the drains, from garden beds and the cracks in roads, a thick, suffocating grey-black mud spilled out. It pooled in gutters, then spread across roads and up over the footpaths and into houses. It flooded through kitchens and living rooms and in some cases flowed up through the floor itself. It came out of the toilets, mixed with sewage. It swallowed gardens and cars and whole suburbs, turning them into toxic, featureless moonscapes.

People knew what it was, technically. The super-fast vibrations of the quake turned the fine topsoil to liquid, and as the heavier soil and rocks churned and sank, the liquid was forced up and out. It's called liquefaction, but it felt like a nightmare. It felt mythical. It was as if the city's fear had been made physically real, and come spilling out of the ground.

After the noise, silence. A frantic kind of silence punctuated by car alarms, the rolling boom of aftershocks, the sharp, vicious clatter of masonry coming down on rescuers. Strangers first, then police, then urban search and rescue teams moved through the city grid, shouting to one another, building-to-building, rubble-to-rubble. The city was declared a no-fly zone so that the search teams' audio equipment could pick up the slightest sound – scratching, tapping, a voice, a breath. It was an incongruous picture: workers poised, almost on tiptoe, listening to the rubble; and at their backs, lines of huge steel diggers, claws upraised, listening too.

The strongest instinct was to get home to family. The city emptied out, but it was a slow and stressful process. The bridges across the Avon were all damaged, and the roads a buckled mess of debris, of mud, of people wandering in shock. I met a woman who ran home to find her children. She had been in the Family Court signing her divorce papers when the quake struck. She and the court clerk flung themselves under the table. *Fuck it*, she thought. She reached back up, grabbed the papers and signed them anyway, though the signature is unlikely to match the one on her licence. When the immediate shocks subsided she ran. She finally got home, 7 kilometres on foot through the mud, and her youngest daughter said, 'What took you so long?'

Many had no homes to go to. Their houses had either collapsed, been thrown off their foundations, were buried in sewage and mud or lacked water, power and shelter from the weather. Hagley Park, where Ngāi Tahu had camped after being removed from their land in the 1850s, once again became a refuge for the displaced.

*

I was in the Australian bush when I got the news. My friend Malcolm said, 'Six point four, in Christchurch. Fatalities, they—' and I was gone, sprinting up the hill to get phone reception. I blundered into a thick spider's web that clung to my face, gummed my eyes and mouth shut. Christchurch was my family, my parents, my brother, grandfather, uncle, cousins, old friends and old flames. It was my memory and my history. I stood in perfect sunshine, and called and called and called. I've never felt so sick.

I went back a month later. The porcelain veneer of Christchurch politeness had cracked with the sewage pipes. As people worked to clear the rubble, they talked. There was a sense of disbelief that could only be whittled away through talking. Underneath each individual story the conversations were the same: people telling each other, over and over, *this is shared*, and *this is real*.

I sat up late one night with Mum in the dining room talking about family, about our own crisis that ran parallel to the earthquakes. She said, 'I don't know what to say,' and the earth said it for her. Thunder rose beneath us, and the shock-wave slammed through, a sickening drag in the guts. It lifted and rolled the floor under our feet and set the house shuddering and moaning in protest. Every object reached a rattling crescendo then the shock passed on and was gone. I was terrified. Mum laughed, not unkindly. 'Four point three, four point four,' she said. 'You'll be okay.' She bounded upstairs to check the GeoNet website. She came back down triumphant. 'Four point four.'

It was a daily game, this filing of earthquakes under precise, knowable numbers, and a small attempt to assert human control. But the aftershocks were so relentless that citizens began displaying the symptoms of extreme stress usually seen in war zones. Grief for people, land and place was setting in. My friend Eric posted on Facebook: 'Um . . . what do we do now?'

I went walking. The city did feel like a war zone. The streets were silent. Once private homes were visible in intimate cross-section, where a fallen wall or chimney had torn open the side of the building. Soldiers in tanks and troop carriers stood guard among the willows and oaks. An older woman with a lip ring asked what the tanks were for. 'We're a tank unit,' insisted the soldier. 'That's just our ride.'

Heading down to Armagh Street and the river, I felt like I had lost the power of speech. So much was gone, and something about the remaining buildings was wrong. They were dreamlike, somehow slumped or bulging, seen through distorted glass. On Armagh Street the Provincial Chambers were as if bombed. My experience and vocabulary were so inadequate that all I could write in my notebook was 'like a large-scale public art installation'.

I came to the Worcester Boulevard bridge, at the centre of a colonial vista running east to the cathedral and west to the museum. This was the apex of the city's conservative heritage, its visual link with the past. It was, as they say, munted. At one end the city founder William Rolleston lay with his head buried in the brickwork. At the other, Godley had toppled like a stiff-legged old drunk. All along this vista and throughout the city, beautiful old heritage buildings had borne the brunt of the damage. They were from the era of colonial arch-conservatism, of tradition and entitlement. The old city's symbol, the Anglican cathedral, had been beheaded.

Beyond the ghosts of an archaic British culture, the streets also contained the personal ghosts of our earlier selves. Looking along Kilmore Street into the cordoned-off Red Zone, I could just see Victoria Square where I spent years as a skater. I imagined myself jumping up onto the bricks, gliding past my mum aged twenty, reading T. S. Eliot on her lunchbreak. From the Caledonian I hear the liquid-glass sounds of free jazz from my dad's band. My grandfather is up by the bridge, a crowd gathered round his open-topped 1936 Opel, the same model that ferried Hitler through the streets of Berlin.

I imagine myself hitting the amphitheatre at speed now. My great-grandmother Emerald Anne, a singer and a gambler, croons an old waiata to herself, waiting outside the courthouse where she translated for Māori prisoners. My wheels blur over the bricks, and as I crouch and launch myself off the stairs, the earthquake hits my imaginings.

Up ahead, the great wide face of the Parkroyal Hotel, where I ate my graduation dinner of bloody lamb, and wondered at the weight of my great-great-grandfather's mortar cap:

it ripples and bulges forward, and its windows shear down
into the amphitheatre. Our Tūāhuriri ancestors are there
below in the old Market Square, blankets about their shoul-
ders, running. I imagine horses screaming in the streets,
and my great-great-grandmother watching as the river, Te
Ōtākaro, devours its banks, and the willows, and its English
name. The European city going under. Stones falling, the
earth opening, a phantom geography of swamp and marshland welling up. Waitaha ancestors calling through the rushes.
All those memories, all the way back, unearthed.

Standing there looking towards Victoria Square, it seemed
to me that the memories bound up in the city were not erased,
but unearthed. They had floated free from the wreckage like
the haze of dust that hung over the city when it all came down.
We were thinking and talking about our own stories, and the
city's histories, as never before. Some would be retained and
re-anchored in the new city. Some, like that thin, high drone of
complacency, had already blown away.

*

Down by Puari Pā, and all along the line of the river Avon, the
geography of the ancestors was still there, just beneath the
surface. In the flooded suburbs, the pre-European landscape
of waterways and marshes was suddenly and terribly visible.

This is a disaster; it is catastrophic, and it is not. Like colonisation, the earthquake means the destruction of the old and
the creation of the new. It marks a symbolic rupture to match
the arrival of Europeans, the break point between one society
and the next. And with the CBD to be rebuilt from the ground
up, there is an opportunity for Ngāi Tahu to re-enter the city,
and a bicultural identity to enter with them.

Ngāi Tahu are, to use an Australian term, the traditional owners of Christchurch. But they are modern capitalist owners as well. Following the iwi's 1997 Treaty settlement the tribe has grown its assets to, at time of writing, $650 million, and is now a heavy hitter in the city's residential and commercial development. Even before the quakes, Ngāi Tahu had bought the central police station, courts, old army barracks and a 50 per cent stake in the council buildings. The tribal leadership has an eye for reliable tenants, and a healthy sense of historic irony. The tribe will be one of the key partners and financial engines of the city's regrowth.

Beyond this economic role is the desire to give voice to iwi values and culture. Key Ngāi Tahu priorities are the enhancement of waterways, indigenous ecosystems and sacred places, and a focus on sustainability and good urban design. The heart of the new city is likely to be a huge bicultural riverfront park, built in partnership with Ngāi Tahu. This is the land where our ancestors gathered, hunted and sang, and may include the old site of Puari Pā. It would be fitting if the response to the current disaster helped break the silence surrounding a much older one.

*

What does Christchurch sound like now? It shifts between the steady murmur of merely surviving the quake – filling buckets with water, rustling through insurance policies – and a healthy cacophony. Much is grief and fear, as people make sense of their loss by sharing it aloud. There is enormous anger too, ultimately caused by the earth, but being vented on those in charge of the clean-up. Civil Defence bulldozers are finishing off unsafe buildings and owners must stand by while their possessions inside are destroyed. In the working-class east, where a cold easterly whips in off the sea, whole suburbs are being written off. This is where most of the city's Māori and Polynesian communities live, and it is a part of Christchurch that has never bought into, or been included in, the city's Englishness. There is a slower, more subtle sense of tragedy unfolding out there, as each street is abandoned house by house.

The cacophony also contains a clear note of determination, and a healthy 'fuck you' to those who would downplay the city's value or the disaster's scale. Remarkable projects like Gap Filler are bringing music, film and creativity back to the city's ruined spaces. Humour is present, too. In response to those who claimed that the first quake's damage to the red-light district proved God hates prostitutes, others have pointed out that the February quake destroyed most of the city's churches. Social connections formed through coping are moving from side effect to centre-stage. Whole streets have become more than just neighbours.

Another aspect of the city's new sound is intimate family conversation, prompted by the act of survival. Christchurch has been a stoic place in the past. Silence has been one of its strongest instincts. At my great-aunt and great-uncle's funeral, a theme was *they were so humble*, and *they never made a fuss*. If there is one thing Christchurch taught its sons and daughters, it was never to make a fuss. But at their funeral I began to learn about the full, difficult, human richness of their lives. The same has happened since the earthquake in February, when people, faced with loss of life and history, have given voice to more family stories.

I have learned about my great-grandfather, who survived World War I, lost everything in the Depression, and was forced to work on his brother's raspberry farm. His bullying at times drove his wife to an asylum. He spent his days shovelling strawberries and raspberries and a swift, sour anger into the vats of jam. His daughter, my great-aunt, made that same jam, but rendered it generous and sweet. I have heard about the Panzer tank that picked off my great-uncle in an Italian field. Shrapnel emerged from his skull decades later. He and his paralysed left arm helped build huts throughout the Southern Alps. I have heard the whisper of melancholia, that most subtle and destructive of tremors, starting with my great-great-great-grandfather who was a guest in the Lyttelton Gaol. The superintendent treated him with books and conversation. Each of these stories tells of disaster; catastrophic, and not. In all of this, I've come to think about resilience and rebuilding.

These myriad conversations have come together in the City Council's Draft City Plan. The cynical nineteen-year-old in me assumed the conservative old city would simply propose a conservative new city, statues, willow trees and all. But, given the chance, Christchurch has collectively proposed something radically different from its old elitist robes. The plan details a green, people-friendly, low-rise, largely car-free space. Ngāi Tahu are front and centre, and the river, Te Ōtākaro, will form a bicultural corridor through the heart of the city.

It is easy to be optimistic from thousands of miles away. The proposal is part design plan, part PR exercise, written while the city is still in collapse. But if even half of the new plan could be achieved, Christchurch would become one of the great little cities of the world. I've never cried over a city council document before. Reading this one, I felt a surge of love and pride. When the city is finally rebuilt, there will be a memorial at its heart. I have a suggestion. It is based on the resonance of the city. I think about the ghostly ringing of the cathedral bells in the first quake. I think about how church bells have rung in times of distress or celebration, and how the wave form of a seismograph resembles the wave form of a piece of music. After all, music and earthquakes are both a type of vibration.

I propose a set of earthquake bells, one for each of the 181 people killed in the February 2011 quake. The bells would be made from the materials of the old city – the bells and organ pipes, the copper roofs and domes. There would be bells of greenstone, and of wood, the materials of the even older settlements. They would range in size from tiny, high and clear all the way down to that biblical, thunderous low C. They would hang in a glistening galaxy beside the ruined cathedral for people to walk among.

Most importantly, the bells would translate the Richter scale into a musical scale. The bells would be played by earthquakes. They would turn the surges of the earth into a strange, exquisite music. The tiny, high-pitched bells would ring almost continuously, a faint flickering sound just on the edge of hearing, a constant reminder not of complacency, but of the living earth. At memorial services, the bells would replay the actual 2010 and 2011 earthquakes, tremor for tremor like a vast symphony. As the vibrations increased, the larger, deeper bells would begin to ring, with great volume and intensity, all the way up to the strikes of the great 6.3 and 7.1 bells. They would transform the power of the earth into a musical, cathartic act of remembrance.

## Megan Clayton
# The Needle and the Damage Done

The wall to the left of the flat, narrow bed was largely clad in boxes labelled 'KITS', that strangely jaunty name for what I assumed were needles, perhaps syringes and whatever sterile, sealed storage their preservation and transport demanded.

The needle whose future work had preoccupied our thinking for the previous four weeks was out of its own kit now, its action calmly described by the consultant who sat near the foot of the bed. Neither my husband nor I saw it; my eyes closed as my husband dropped his head toward the floor, knees and feet splayed and hands clasped in the sad stock pose of the waiting man.

The incursion of the needle was less painful than a blood test or an injection: with almost no sensation through the skin and then with resistance through the uterine wall, which contracted, as predicted, dully and at its distant perimeter.

Baby's fine, said the consultant, and far away from the needle. Not paying any attention at all. All done for now.

All done: that moment's marker that refers only to the passing of that incident, the completing of that process, in this case the step toward another degree of certainty at which, we were assured, we – I – would feel better, or at least less wretched. The process to this point had been a mélange of measurements and statistical probabilities, calculated from

First published on Megan's blog Harvest Bird, 27 December 2011
(http://archive.harvestbird.com/2011/12/27/the-needle-and-the-damage-done/).

a wider range of sources than when I was pregnant with my first daughter two years earlier. Some were tangible and some painfully speculative. All pointed toward what felt, every day, like a door about to close behind me.

I had mantras, straws at which to clutch, that worked for some of the time. In moments of lucidity I could laugh at their disparate origins. A partly remembered maxim from a former counsellor: that the ability to cope with uncertainty is a sign of mental health. The cricketer Viv Richards, murmuring to the interviewer in the documentary *Fire in Babylon* that 'I always backed myself'. Back yourself to raise this baby, I murmured in turn, not actually saying it out loud, but imagining myself speaking through gritted teeth. The universal message of my colleagues, that they thought us best equipped among parents to take care of a child with the disability the numbers offered us. People wouldn't consistently say that just to be *nice*, I reasoned, even in a workplace culture that prizes niceness above many other things.

I read multiple scholarly and newspaper articles to try to better understand just what our numbers were saying, grimly mindful too of the phrase 'our numbers' and its usual location in fortune, lottery, fate. I did so much reading and research that I was instructed by more than one social service not to do any more.

Of the fetuses whose nuchal fold – an area at the back of the neck – was measured at the end of the first trimester, just 5 per cent of those called normal would have a measurement greater than 2.5 millimetres. Of the fetuses who would be born with Down syndrome or other conditions caused by chromosomal variations (I found the standard phrase 'abnormality' almost intolerable to say), almost all would have a nuchal fold measurement greater than 2.5 millimetres. Our fetus had a measurement of 3.6 millimetres. Measuring alone could not indicate to which of the two groups a fetus with a larger measurement belonged. The odds could be further refined by including blood test results, maternal age and maternal weight in the calculation. This done, we had learned at the beginning of the thirteenth week of pregnancy that the particular set of odds given our fetus were one in five of having trisomy 21, which causes Down syndrome. The odds for the other trisomic conditions, rarer and more disabling, were also increased, but none to that extent.

It was strange to have a private drama take over our daytime thoughts in a year where all dramas and the source of collective hardship had been public, civic and seismological; and the reminder to self to think of the unhappiness of Christchurch's eastern suburbs, to put my own uncertainty into some wider and more worthy context, was another of my daily maxims. These stuck as inconsistently as a fridge magnet thrown at a metal door from a distance. (It was further undermined when a colleague from the eastern suburbs told me she was using my worries to keep her own earthquake-related problems in perspective.)

I write of fears and worries, but these were specific. I was worried about our ability to take care of a child with disabilities, when the nature of those disabilities remained unknown, except under the wide umbrella of a syndrome: developmental delays and cognitive limitations reduced in significance by the fact of a first-year mortality rate of 15 per cent for affected children; the fear of prejudice, the fear of domestic chaos. I was also, far more pressingly, worried about my ability to know my own mind, my own wishes, in a system which included the facilitation of swift, early termination of such a fetus. My anguish was widely read as good grounds for abortion, should our particular trisomy be confirmed. I did not want this, but nor did I want the anguish.

The fact that we were a minority in this projected path – my reading suggested that anywhere between 70 and 80 per cent of fetuses confirmed with trisomy 21 are aborted – made trusting that I wanted to choose this path even more distressing. It put me in conflict with my husband, into whose moral philosophy relativism has made considerably fewer insinuations than mine. That first emotional plumb, the sounding at the first scan that we wanted our baby regardless, sustained him in a way it did not me. What if I were wrong about our abilities, our commitment? Neatly and swiftly, my fear that this would tear us apart did an accelerated job of doing just that, our lives over those four weeks converted by bitter irony and meta-narrative into a functioning version of what I feared would happen in future, and all, as my husband pointed out, for a paper tiger, a fetus whose nature remained unknown to us.

So I had amniocentesis, the narrative needle to extract the fluid in which chromosomes could be counted. After forty-eight hours and then again at two weeks those odds that more than one professional had described as 'huge' were revealed to have gone our way, in that our fetus – female, who quickly became to us a girl, a daughter – had no trisomies, no syndrome, none of our fears. In the relief of this news persisted the fear of the increased risk of miscarriage that came with the procedure, the shadow of a shadow that we had also wondered how we might endure. Roulette, said my husband, Russian roulette; but my mental health was not going to hold up with the alternative, without amniocentesis, of six months of waiting. Between us we found enough emotional capital – wedding vows; the memory of our beloved grandparents, so loyal to each other – to wear that fear.

What do we have now? We have our eighteen-week-old fetus, the daughter-to-be, longed for no less during the month-long possibility of those trisomies, and her older sister, and each other. We have the possibility of fetal heart problems, another spectre of that larger nuchal measurement, at the coming anatomy scan. We have angry, radicalised, idealised sensibilities, the strong notion that society needs to change, that the solution to fetuses conceived with trisomies is not necessarily or logically that they not be born. The fact that this is the chosen path for so many parents of these fetuses speaks to me of a wider environment in which those commonplace concerns of feminism and the history of labour are dominant.

The way in which the demands of work and family are positioned as fundamentally in competition, rather than in alignment with each other, the way in which the development of children is predicated, even before they are born, on their ability one day to join the industrialised workforce, the way in which the value of people is quantified to some degree by the amount of money their thriving will cost the state: all these things contribute to a normalising and privileging of certain kinds of human over others. Guidelines for those contemplating carrying or not carrying a fetus with a trisomy invite them to consider such questions as what the value of life might be, as if these are matters best reflected on by strained, frightened parents in a window of just a few weeks. Why should the work of moral philosophy devolve to those in personal crisis, while the rest of the community rehearses at leisure arguments of public utility?

It pains me to impose upon the cool brisk tone I like to bring to my written work something approaching an impassioned plea, but these are moral questions for us all, and we have a social duty, I believe, to push beyond the post-industrial dictates of neo-liberalism, to find, as the writer and mother Robin Hyde argued in the 1930s, the way forward for a society in which mothers (and now fathers too) can work and have their children, including disabled children. In the present era, the standing social prescription for the young disabled is both coy and oblique, centred on the story of their diminished prospects as contributors to the national economy. Ways to counteract this narrative are few, and turn in the main on the notion of private good: familial love. Love as cipher, love as slogan, a thing hard to measure against the prevailing notion of our shared accountability.

I do not think the social value of my unborn daughter ought to be contingent on the fact that she will not be born with the trisomy that causes Down syndrome. I do not think our wish to bear and raise her even had this been true should be regarded as an aberrant choice. I do not think anyone is helped in this by narrow abortion laws that make a fetus with disabilities just one of a few reasons for which a pregnancy may not legally continue, although on this matter I doubt I have any stomach for engaging in internet debate.

It is easy when living and working the life of the mind, when running a household of little conflict and relative privilege not to think in any personal manner about the wider state systems that sustain and shape our moral choices, our assumptions about the value and viability of life. The current structures of our social and medical bureaucracies collude to make this thinking the work of others. It is not the community but the affected individuals who are left to contend with the consequences of their crisis-to-hand: the disappearing job, the sick or disabled family member, the misbegotten fetus. Our experience has brought my husband and me into immediate, visceral contact with those questions, in a manner that exposes a wider lack of social vocabulary to consider them outside of economic utility or personal choice. It brings us to that umbrella question that is the go-to for the left-wing view: if it is like this for us, then how is it for others? On this and in this, as much as in the increasing fetal movement of my growing daughter-to-be, my thinking turns.

# Naomi Arnold
## Mother's Day

Mum arrived to live with us on Valentine's Day. She'd packed her beloved juicer, her favourite bed linen, a photo of her grandmother, and the good kitchen knives.

'Not the good knives,' her partner said when she left him, but she took them anyway. She abandoned the town where she'd spent her entire life and drove eight hours south, down the spine of the North Island. In Wellington, she drove up the ramp of the *Awatere*, the ferry that crosses rough Cook Strait to the drowned green valleys of the top of the south. As she left northern soil, her mobile phone grew hot, and died. She took it as a sign. As signs go, it was a powerful one, but somewhat inconvenient considering she hadn't told anyone she was going, couldn't remember her email password, wasn't on Facebook and didn't have anyone's contact details written down. When her friends rang home, her partner told them she'd left, and that was that. As far as they could tell, she had simply vanished.

When she reached Nelson, Mum unpacked her bags into my spare upstairs room, made up the bed with her best linen, put the good knives in the kitchen drawer, the juicer into the top cupboard, and tacked her grandmother's photograph to the bedroom wall. During the next two weeks, she drank too much wine and cooked Thai green curries and roast chickens

First published in *Ten Spurs: The Best of the Best from the Mayborn Literary Nonfiction Conference*, vol. 7 (Frank W. Mayborn Graduate Institute of Journalism, University of North Texas, 2014); and winner of the Mayborn Literary Nonfiction Contest, Texas, July 2013.

and an enormous heavy carrot cake, and then another one just
to perfect it. Scones, with butter and cream and jam. I gained
3 kilograms.

Up north, her friends and family began to murmur, and
worry. They couldn't reach her, so they found me, and I began
to field phone calls, emails and Facebook messages.

'Where is yer ma currently?' my uncle messaged me a few
days after she arrived.

'She's here,' I said. 'And she's okay. She brought her juicer.'

'Tell her to check our mum's headstone proof on her email
cos I need to approve it. Urgent.'

I rang my home number.

'Hi. Ring your brother,' I said when she answered. 'Or
remember your email password. He needs to approve
Grandma's headstone.'

'Oh God,' she said. 'I can't be bothered.'

'I really need to get it sorted after back and forth hassles for
eight months,' my uncle typed. 'I think I've put the frighteners
up the arse of the mason. Ha!'

'He says he's put the frighteners up the arse of the stone-
mason,' I said.

'I bet he has,' she said. 'Tell him whatever he puts is fine by
me.'

'She says whatever you put is fine by her,' I wrote. My phone
beeped; she'd texted her favourite old Spike Milligan joke.
So I typed: 'She says to make sure the mason puts "I told you I
was ill!" at the bottom.'

'Oh, very good,' he said.

It was no wonder she wanted to escape. There had been the
long illnesses and deaths of her parents, drawn out over years.
Her father had finally succumbed to cancer after months in a
rest-home bed. He resisted it as long as he could, and when he

moved in he said of his catatonic fellow inmates: 'They're all old. They're dying.' The end did not take long after that.

In his last days, he joked to his four gathered children that his Scottish ancestry was sending him off before the government introduced its plan to hike taxes. But we only found this out afterwards. As the end came, he refused to let his grandchildren see him, alive or dead, and forbade Mum to even tell us the state he was in. Instead, she called one day and told us we'd better come up to say goodbye. When we got there, we discovered he had already left. He'd wanted to preserve our memories of him whole and cancer free, to guard us against the bleak shock of death.

A couple of years later, Mum's mother wore out and died tidily, slipping away without a fuss in the night. In her last year she had roused herself only for the rest-home tea trolley, though her cheeks always burned a bright pink; and when I was home for visits I pretended to myself that although she couldn't speak or smile, the crinkled skin next to her eyes meant she knew me.

She died on 12 May 2012 – Mum's fifty-fourth birthday, which that year also happened to be the day before Mother's Day. 'I'm an orphan,' she said when she told me.

And so Mum escaped to me, her oldest daughter. She bought rugs for my house. She bought us identical scarves. She furnished us with curtains, and spent a sunny afternoon laughing with the man who came to hang them, who swore blind that he was a direct descendent of Goethe and in fact that all Goethe's direct living descendants were Māori New Zealanders, like him.

She held phone conversations with her abandoned partner long into the night, her strident voice echoing through our wooden floors. She spent evening hours ranting, violently shaking out laundry and folding it, diagnosing him over and over with Asperger's syndrome, convinced it was the root of their problems; and when I read up about it and told her about a line that said: 'At some point in their lives, every woman will think her man has Asperger's,' she could only laugh, helplessly.

And she fell in love with Nelson, my adopted home. She found peace in the close cosy hills to the east and the long shallow sands of Farewell Spit to the west, where seabirds swooped and whorled like fluttering pieces of paper tossed from an unseen hand. Ours is a city the big jets fly over, leaving its blue skies striped with white contrails on a high, clear day. It's a city crazy enough that a good chunk of its population are convinced those white streaks are chemtrails, biological or chemical weapons sprayed by the United States Government to keep New Zealanders passive, like hobbits. It's a city beautiful enough that people give up everything to move here, or to stay.

Mum found the best coffee shops, bought one of those granny carts on wheels and marched to the markets on Saturday mornings, returning home with it filled with vegetables and half a bag of crisp Italian doughnuts – she'd eaten the rest. She went to the gym and started art classes, obsessively rendering her pencil sketches, over and over.

'Is this any good?' she said, and showed me a sketch of her grandmother, taken from the photograph.

'Yes!' I said.

'Nah. I've overcooked it,' she said, and quickly flipped the sketchbook closed.

In coming here she was treading a path I had made four years ago. When I left her and my home up north I went to university without looking back, and then moved from New Zealand to Australia to South Korea and back to New Zealand, from job to job – until in 2009 I landed, floundering, at a friend's place in Christchurch. I spent the next six months chasing money, bruised and tired from a year of trying to escape a doomed relationship. That winter, I arrived in Nelson to a new job – and, enraptured, stayed.

I loved living under the black night skies, salted with stars that hung so close over the rooflines it seemed you could float up and swim through them. I loved seeing the thousands of starlings that swooped as one over the harbour when the sky relaxed from hard blue to softest pink, and knowing I was in the top of the south, at the beginning of the magnificent spine of these shaky isles, cradled in the curve of a bay bordered with such untrammelled wilderness that people disappear in it every summer, and cavers are still plumbing its deep passages. There are no killer animals in New Zealand. It is the land that will swallow you whole.

But I found peace in the hiking trails, mountain tops, and fingernails of sandy beach washed over at high tide. And at the end of my third year I found Doug, another emotional refugee, struggling with depression and a divorce that robbed him of his family, a home with his two young children, and just about everything else. Though neither of us was looking, though it was a terrible idea, we began to spin a delicate web which only grew stronger as sorrow, shame and fear broke over him night after night. As a new father, he had loved to carry his daughter out into the navy-blue night to point out the stars and the moon. She rewarded him with one of her first words: 'star'. But that was back when he still had a family. He did not get that chance with his son.

We needed a place to rest. So I scraped together every cent and bought my first house, found for me by Ben, a friend who lived on the same street. We didn't know then, but we moved in on the same night Grandma took her last breaths in her

rest-home bed up north, and woke up in the morning to find
the world slightly altered.

My father, newly happy in Australia, bought us a fridge
and a washing machine as housewarming presents. Slowly,
we smoothed the wrinkles of our anxiety. Doug carved up
the back hillside with a spade and created flat spaces for his
children to play, and learned to build dry stone walls to hold
back the slip of the land. He built vegetable beds and compost
bins, and found a brazier made from an old washing machine
barrel. He used tin snips to cut out shapes of a rocket ship,
stars and the moon, so his daughter could poke marshmal-
lows through the holes to roast, and watch the flames leaping
up into the night.

Slowly, as March turned to April, and the first red oak
leaf fluttered to the ground across the street, Mum and her
partner came to an agreement, and Doug's children came to
stay. On the second to last night before Mum headed back,
he walked grinning through the front door, carrying both
his daughter and son, their overnight bags dangling from his
elbows. Mum fed them toast and spaghetti, cut up carrots,
and offered them ice cream. Later, we did the dishes and
watched through the kitchen window as he carried his solemn
little boy outside to look at the night sky and whisper to him
about the moon and the stars.

On her last night, Mum presided over an extravagant three-
course dinner party held for my neighbours – including Ben,
who'd found me our house.

'Hey,' he said, as we sat in the living room eating chips.
'That house at the end of the street is for sale.'

Mum said, 'What?'

She flew home the next morning, leaving the car, her
juicer, the good knives, her favourite linen, the photo of her

grandmother. She got back up north in time to reconnect with her partner and consider their next step, and to attend the memorials of some of those she had lost.

Then I got a phone call.

'Can you go and take a few photos of that house at the end of the street for me? I want to put an offer on it.'

'But you haven't seen it! Have you organised it with the tenants?'

'Noo . . . just sneak up and snap a few, would you? Go on.'

I did better than that. I squelched up in the rain and shot a video showing off the native trees, the grand deck, a peek of the living room through rain-splattered windows, and the quarter acre of unkempt garden.

'I could do wonders with that!' she squealed when she saw it.

And so it was that my mother bought a matching house nine doors up. It is butter-yellow and high on the hillside, basking in the strong clear sunlight and sporting wonderful views of the ocean from every room. That is, we presume it does. We have yet to get inside to find out.

This will be just the second place she has lived in her entire life, and after fourteen years apart, we'll be together again. I wonder if she sensed before I did that there might be new children arriving here soon, waiting until we are ready to welcome them – and that she is doing what she can to blend us all into something approximating a family. New and fragile, but a family all the same.

Greg Bruce

# The Desperate Quest: How Auckland's Property Market Drove Me to the Edge of Insanity

This is how fast it happened: at the beginning of the week, we were happy renters, without the desire or ability to buy a house. Then somebody posted a link on Twitter, we looked at some pictures, and a few days later we were standing with an agent in the kitchen of a house in Kelston, caring about nothing so much as owning that house.

It was a plain old three-bedroom weatherboard place on a rambling section that would be perfect for the family we would be starting six months hence, except for the fact that we had no interest in buying a house and even less interest in buying a house in Kelston.

The area didn't look nice. No self-respecting agent would even say it looked like it was coming up. But the house was down a private driveway and it was on the water – a mangrove swamp if you really want to be a dick about it – and once you were on the back deck, it could have been miles from anywhere. It wasn't – it was in Kelston – but once the idea of your own home has sucked you into its world of possibilities, reality is as nothing to you.

So there we were. We had no more money than a few days earlier, when we were hardly rich enough to rent our existing

First published in *Metro*, October 2013.

tiny flat, but the thought of owning that place suddenly filled us with strange, unjustified dreams of a brighter future.

By most measures, this was the middle of the least affordable property market in history. But you get the property market you deserve, or at least the one your parents' generation created for you, and you say, 'Well, everybody's in the same boat!' and you prepare to plunge into crippling debt because everyone you know tells you to, because they have.

And although the *Herald* and others sometimes run confusing columns on why it's sometimes better to rent, you can't be expected to understand them, or to believe them, in the face of all that well-meaning advice.

We went back to the Kelston open home the following weekend, possibly even the following two weekends, with our parents. I got a QV report telling me the house's selling range would be $380,000 to $450,000.

We met a mortgage broker at a hastily arranged lunch meeting on Ponsonby Road and bought her an organic cola. She told us that based on my wife's income and the fact we had a deposit, we could borrow an implausible amount of money. She didn't mention my income and I think the implication was that we never should.

We sent her some information and a few days later we were pre-approved to buy a house for up to $550,000. It was a scaled-down version of the original implausible figure, but still we decided not to buy anything approaching it, figuring it would imprison us in a debt from which we would likely never escape.

The auction was at Barfoot & Thompson's Shortland Street auction rooms on a weekday morning – I think a Friday. It was a pleasantly appointed room, crammed with more than a hundred people, and our property was first on the block.

Where bidding started, I can't remember, because it moved at a terrifying pace through the 400,000s, where we were willing to bid, and into the 500,000s, where any meaningful measure of value became irrelevant. Eventually two bidders remained: an older couple sitting directly behind me, and a middle-aged man standing at the back of the room.

As bidding hit the 600s, the older guy said to his wife: 'Who is it?' She looked back, and whispered something about the other guy. 'Fuck!' he said, and raised the aggression of his bidding, thrusting his hand in the air, increasing his bid multiples.

But none of that mattered because the middle-aged man at the back just kept his hand in the air and never put it down, never wavered. What figure would he have gone to? I doubt he cared. At the ridiculous figure of $652,000, the older couple walked out and he was the new owner of a small, swampy, overpriced corner of Kelston.

I walked out of the auction and found Shortland Street looking strange and different. Reality seemed to have come slightly unmoored. I recognised a young, professional couple crossing the road ahead of me. They had been early bidders on the Kelston property. I asked them what they thought about paying $652,000 for a property in Kelston. They thought it was crazy. 'I think it's an anomaly,' she said. I wanted to believe her.

That should have been it, in theory. We had not been interested in buying a property; we had become interested in buying a property; we had discovered that property to be massively beyond our means. The next logical step was to return to our uninterested equilibrium.

But the world of property is no respecter of logic. Not only were we now interested in property, we were consumed by it.

It wasn't that we were blinded to the potential problems. Hardly a week went by in the next few fevered months when I didn't say to Zanna, 'What are we doing trying to buy in the most overheated property market in history?' or similar.

Hardly a week went by without me forwarding her some cautionary *Herald* article about why it was a bad time to buy. But still, no weekend went by without us driving to a cavalcade of open homes, scrawling price estimates, possibilities, problems across our sheets of Trade Me print-outs.

We had been married for a few months; our first baby was on the way. We had a long and hopeful future spread before us. We imagined that future intimately and decided it would be in Te Atatū. Why did we make that decision? I don't know. Like so many of the decisions we made during that period, our justifications seemed to be post hoc and flimsy. We knew a few people out there and had already looked at a couple of places, so we had some tiny idea of the area's value. It seemed like the most central place we could afford. It had shops.

The first Te Atatū place we became really interested in was at the end of a delightful cul-de-sac. The name of the street was also Zanna's uncle's name and the number was the number of my childhood home. It had a lovely flat lawn and fruit trees. It had a shed and a strange but pleasant conservatory. These weren't things that we were necessarily looking for, but once we saw them, they absolutely were.

It quickly became the only house we had ever wanted. The agent said interest had been in the 400s. I went to the auction. It was at the Barfoot & Thompson offices in Shortland Street. Interest was quickly apparent beyond the 400s and into the high 500s, setting a pattern we would see repeated again and again: agents would tell you interest was at one level, your hopes would rise, then the property would sell for an extra $100,000 or more. We came to learn that, 'It will probably have a four in it,' came with the unspoken rider, 'If it's still 1998.'

You would think we would have just recalibrated and started looking at cheaper properties. But we didn't. Have you ever looked at the type of place that 'will probably have a three in it'? It's fine to sit there high and mighty and say first-home buyers have to adjust their expectations, but do you understand how much adjustment is involved here?

It's a tough argument, because you don't want to look like the person quoted recently in the *Herald* who said prices are so ridiculous that she had been reduced to looking in West Auckland. It's a question of what's reasonable.

The median price of Auckland dwellings was \$272,000 in 2003. By the middle of 2013, it was \$562,000 and rising steadily. Over the past year alone, median prices had risen 12 per cent. What is the logic to that? How is that reasonable?

Early in 2013, the ninth annual Demographia International Housing Affordability Survey showed Auckland housing prices to be 6.7 times the city's median household income. Anything over five is considered 'severely unaffordable'. There is no category above 'severely unaffordable'. Of all the world-wide cities in the study with over a million people, only nine had a higher median multiple.

As our search went on, I quoted figures and studies like this to Zanna with such regularity that I think she grew to despise me.

'Greg thinks we're in a bubble,' she said to her father over dinner one night, presumably in the hope he would dismiss my concerns.

'We are,' he said.

'He thinks it's going to burst,' she said.

'That's probably right too,' he said.

Battling within me were two fears. I feared that if we bought at that time, we would be buying just before the market died, leaving us financially exposed. But I also feared that if we didn't buy at that time the exploding market would leave us behind, with even less chance of being able to afford a decent place to live.

There appeared no way out. My life became an endless cycle of emailed Trade Me alerts, prodigious open-home schedules and early-week follow-up phone calls from real estate agents. We would go to open homes, hear sweet lies about expected value, go to the auction anyway, watch bidding spiral beyond us, walk out into the Dalí-esque atmosphere of a city that had come unhinged from the idea of inherent value, and we would start again.

For whatever reason, I never felt completely hopeless, which in some ways made it worse. There was always the feeling that this particular open home might be the one where nobody appreciates the value and we could sneak in a lowball offer only a slightly ridiculous amount above its actual value. But the longer we spent in the market, the more obvious it became that this was crazy thinking for which there was no evidence. It was the same logic that leads people to believe they will one day win the lottery.

But Oprah has always said that if you put something out to the universe you get something back, and although I have never believed that to be true, a long spell in the Auckland property market will make you reconsider many things.

This was the context in which – some months into our search – the email arrived. A family member had seen a property they wanted to help us buy. It would be a partnership thing. It was a nice, small 1980s three-bedroom brick house in a nice neighbourhood, on a smallish section. Although it was neither the type of house nor the type of location we had been interested in, it quickly became everything we had ever wanted and the only place in which we had ever wanted to live.

We found a list of recent sales in the neighbourhood and, based on those, we calculated what we thought it would go for. Something in the early 800s seemed likely. Finance was sorted and our lawyer looked over the title and other legal stuff. It all looked good. At the final open home, we got a ladder and checked the gutters.

I went to the auction. It was at Barfoot & Thompson in Shortland Street. I found myself standing with an agent. He encouraged me to start the bidding, which I refused to do until I found myself doing it, at $780,000. The room turned to me. I felt proud and terrified.

For a long time, nobody countered and I entertained the thought of drinking champagne at my new breakfast bar later that night, but that hope died with the sound of the auctioneer calling $800,000. Such a simple thing, the raising of a hand, the calling of a number: it was hard to believe there could be so much weight behind it.

'If you're serious, come right back at him,' the agent whispered to me. Was I serious? I was beginning to doubt it. I raised my hand anyway. '820,' said the auctioneer, pointing at me. Our limit was 840, maybe 850 if it looked like we might get it by stretching.

Barely was my hand down when the auctioneer pointed across the room and called 840. He looked immediately back at me, as did the rest of the room, and he asked for 860. Seconds before, I had bid at 780. I knew this was how auctions worked, but not that this was how they felt.

I shook my head and looked at my feet, ashamed and disappointed. Immediately, somebody else bid at 860. Seconds later, somebody else said 900. New bidders entered, several of them, people who had not even bothered bidding until my piddling limit had been passed.

$995,000 it sold for. Who got it, I don't know. I left into the murky morning, wondering how we suddenly had double the amount of money to play with, but just as little prospect of buying a house.

But of course I knew. It didn't matter whether we had $400,000 or $1 million to spend, if we felt a house was overvalued, we weren't prepared to buy it, and it seemed increasingly obvious that everything was overvalued: the unprecedented rise in prices over the past decade, the outrageous median multiple of 6.7, the open homes swarmed by rabid buyers, the endless bringing forward of auctions because of the exorbitant pre-auction offers.

In describing my consumer persona, Zanna recently told a friend: 'He's constantly afraid that everybody is trying to pull his pants down when he's not looking.' This is a true statement, but in the Auckland property market, it looks to me like the only way to buy a property is with your pants down.

But no matter how strongly I felt about the overheated market and the fact we would never find something we deemed reasonable value, I didn't want to stop looking. Because, as real estate agents understand and never tire of mentioning, you buy homes with your emotions.

When I looked at a house, I imagined my future children laughing and playing on the lawn. I imagined parties on the deck and tearful episodes of future television soaps in the lounge. I created memories in advance and I fell in love.

Love is nothing though. In a market like this one, where you can turn up to an open home ten minutes early and still struggle to park your car, and where you can reasonably expect to have to queue in the hallway to get a look at the bathroom, the more powerful emotion is fear: fear that you'll never get into a house, that these hordes of open-homers are all richer than you, are prepared to offer more than you, are more desperate than you. And those people are thinking the same thing about you.

I'm not saying that fear is necessarily the driver behind this crazed market we're in, but nor am I saying it isn't.

By the time we'd missed out on the $995,000 property, Zanna was nearly seven months pregnant. The idea of moving house and setting up started to seem too difficult, and gave us a reason to break the cycle that I believe would otherwise have driven us to do what it seemed like so many of the city's young families had done – engage in a debt that was far beyond reasonable, for a house that didn't warrant it.

We agreed that we would start looking again when our baby is old enough for us to again take regular showers. Part of me hopes we don't, but that's my rational side. Part of me fears that my rational side will be overruled. Part of me hopes that it will. Part of me doesn't know what's rational any more.

Steve Braunias
# About an Egging

Even before the night of the eggs I had a feeling that we weren't welcome in the neighbourhood. It was only a theory and I didn't put a lot of store in it. It dated back to the day we bought the house at auction. I'd walked to the nearby shops and bought a pie and a doughnut to celebrate. I looked around at the trees, the sky, the view of pale water. Everything was fresh and appealing, and so were the pastries, which I scoffed on the pavement on a quiet, sunny morning in spring. I felt at peace. I'd arrived. A car drove past and the driver yelled out, 'Weirdo!'

I stood rooted to the spot in my Ugg boots and knee-length winter coat with a scorch mark on it. My mouth hung open until I filled it with the doughnut. I trudged across the road, got in the car and slammed the door. I wanted to cry. A line from a poem by Sylvia Plath rattled around inside my head: 'The villagers never liked you . . .'

Well, no fears for steady men. I got over it. Two months later came the night of the eggs; it took a bit longer, but I got over that, too, or thought I had, until my daughter, who wore what I fancied was a dreamy expression on her lovely face, turned to me in the middle of the day in the middle of summer, and said, 'Do you remember when we got egged?'

Summer was ruined. Her words touched me like a bolt of lightning, and everything went dark. I felt cold. I felt afraid.

First published in *Metro*, March 2013.

An ancient grief had returned. 'Yes,' I said, in a faraway voice, 'I remember.'

It was two years ago. She was four. She was shocked; we all were, standing on the balcony and staring at the yellow chaos on the outside of our sliding glass doors. It was Sunday morning. We were in our pyjamas. My daughter said, 'What happened?'

Violence, mysterious and brutal, had intruded on our blameless suburban lives. Three eggs had been thrown with some force. They hit the glass at roughly my daughter's height, and dribbled down the glass in thick, sticky lines. They ended at the eggshells, which lay broken and tender on the balcony. The cat sniffed at the glass, and licked it. I shoved it away with my foot, and said, 'Don't.'

The fourth egg – there's always a fourth egg in crime narratives – had been dropped on the street below. It pinpointed the likely spot where the culprit or culprits had stood when they looked up and let fly. 'Why did the egg,' I wondered, 'cross the road?'

\*

Was it random, was it calculated, was it sending a message? I felt the eyes of the street on my back all that morning as I cleaned up the mess. It took ages. The yolk had hardened on the glass, suggesting the eggs hadn't been thrown the night before – they'd had time to stiffen, and grip to the glass like glue. Probably the assailant or assailants unknown had looked at the mess in the past few days and laughed his or her or their stupid head or heads off. Probably it was happening right now as I used sponges, hot water, rags, paper towels, Jif, Lux, Windolene and bad language.

Who, and why? I drew up a list of likely suspects. It started with the family across the road. Hunched and bearded, they seem beyond number, five or maybe six generations under four or five roofs, with ten or eleven trucks always parked on the front lawn, and not a single tree or even a shrub to conceal their feral arrangement. We don't speak, not since I approached the tribe's matriarch when she was at the letterbox, and called out heartily, 'Gidday there!' I sounded like a good joker. But the whiskery old crone simply collected her mail, turned on her walking stick, and hobbled inside the house.

What was her problem? But I knew the answer. Issues of race and income shadowed our every step. The whitening of west and south Auckland is a modern phenomenon; waves of middle-class and relatively affluent Europeans have moved there as first-home buyers, as different and as startling as Africans. The disruptions to the old order have inevitably led to tensions. On quiet nights, I can hear the neighbourhood seething, and my own heart beating.

What about the character two doors down? He was next on the list. Severely paranoid, he lives alone behind a 2-metre-high corrugated barricade with barbed wire, whirring security cameras and a mad dog. His car has blacked-out windows. I've only seen him twice on the street. I called out heartily, 'Gidday there!' He turned, and fled.

What about the brute with an afro who walks the streets at night? In some neighbourhoods, what he's doing is known as exercise, but he looks capable of anything.

What about the old guy who walks the streets in daylight? Not me, the other old guy. He walks to the dairy three or four times a day, back and forth, desperate for company. He doesn't look capable of much, but you never know.

What about the family next door? When we moved in, they baked us a cake. It was delicious. Their kids play with our daughter all the time. The parents attend church. In short, they were just as likely to have thrown the eggs as anyone else.

*

The list grew with each new face, but I never got to the bottom of it. I tried to put it out of my mind. 'Weirdo!', the egging – these things happen. It was best to keep things in perspective, and not take it personally. If I felt unwelcome, then the point was to turn things around, and become part of the community.

I sort of have. I do things at my daughter's school. I judged the speech contest, cooked sausages at the gala and helped out with literacy classes – I know the names of maybe thirty, forty kids. For the first time in my adult life, I've felt like I belong to where I live.

The mangroves, the stilts on the mudflats, the light above the water in the afternoons. There is the menswear shop and there is the ice-cream parlour. There are the woods where I collect pinecones, and there is the playground where I take my daughter and her best friend and we play crocodiles.

Lovely. Underneath that fine and pleasant veneer, though, has been the dark stain of the incident of the eggs in the night-time. It all came spluttering and fizzing to the surface when my daughter asked if I remembered it.

The trauma returned, and so did the mystery. Who did it? Who sent that message, who made that emphatic, yellow statement on our glass sliding doors? My daughter, so apparently serene as she stood on the balcony in the middle of the day in the middle of summer, looked at me and said, 'Who do you think it was?'

Perhaps I was looking at it the wrong way. Maybe I needed to look at the other end of the telescope. I always had a feeling that the answer lay in the fourth egg.

What if it didn't, in fact, mark where the eggs had been thrown?

What if it had been thrown from the balcony?

She said, 'What are you thinking?'

The last thing I investigated on the morning we discovered the egging was to conduct a stocktake of our cupboards.

She said, 'Have you thought of who it was?'

It didn't cross my mind that we might have been short by four eggs. It didn't strike me as revealing that the impact of the thrown eggs was roughly my daughter's height. But it did occur to me that you can't trust anyone.

She said, 'Why are you looking at me like that?'

Her face was as smooth as an egg.

## Leilani Tamu
# Notes on Cultural Diplomacy

### 1. The Window

I was twelve when I first ran away from home. I remember sitting in front of the window in my sister's room, wondering if I could do it. Could I climb out and breach the 6-metre gap between the window and the grass verge below? I remember sitting there for what seemed like hours, contemplating the different spaces I would need to navigate: out the narrow window, across the grass verge, over the back fence and into the dark streets of Auckland. Headed somewhere, nowhere, anywhere, but there.

Now, in my thirties, I'm amazed that I had the guts to take the first step. Age seems to have brought about reason, but reason tinged with an undercurrent of fear. I've become the adult I never understood. At twelve, fear was pointless. At thirty, fear is a necessity. And, for me, that window marks the point of transition. In crossing that space, I created a platform for a new-found consciousness. One that was liberating at first and terrifying in the end. Now every time I look at that window I'm reminded of that night, of that moment in my life. And whenever my three-year-old daughter stays in

Part 1 of this piece was previously published in *Lead Us Outside, Lead Us Quietly*, catalogue for an exhibition of Talia Smith's photographs of forgotten spaces, 16 April 2014 (Wellington: Enjoy Gallery, 2014); part 5, 'Mouths Wide Shut', is from an article first published in *Metro*, October 2012; and parts 2–4 first appeared on Leilani's blog Cultural Diplomacy (http://culturaldiplomacyblog.com/), November 2013 and May 2014.

that room, my first instinct is to close the blinds: to protect her from what lies on the other side of that space.

## 2. Let's Talk About Sex

We all know the song: 'Let's talk about sex, baby/ let's talk about you and me . . .' Salt-n-Pepa shook it up 'real good'; it doesn't matter what generation you're coming from, you're likely to have heard it. And I bet those Roast Buster boys were pretty familiar with it too. That's right, this is about sex. The ugly side of sex. Sexual assault. Sexual abuse. Rape. The things we don't talk about often enough. The side of sex that every person in New Zealand has to come to terms with at some point in their journey. Whether directly or indirectly. It affects us all. And because I haven't met every person in New Zealand, I can only draw on the painful, bitter truth that is my experience. So brace yourself. This isn't going to be an easy read.

*The year is 1995. I am thirteen years old. A guy I have a crush on asks me to meet him at the back of the library after school one day. I turn up. I'm excited. I really like this guy. He's three years older than me. He's handsome. He's popular. I have hopes that he's going to ask me out. And he does. He says he likes me too. He really wants to date me. But he wants me to meet a friend first. He walks me to the park around the corner. Takes me down a path that leads into some bushes. There are other boys there. He has a knife . . . and you can figure out the rest.*

For over fifteen years now I have lived with this experience, kept it hidden, tried to pretend like it never happened. Why?

Because for so long I felt guilty. Felt dirty. Felt ashamed. Felt like it was my fault that I got myself into that situation. My parents had warned me about the risks I was taking. But I was a rebel, you see. The fia poto (know-it-all) teenager who thought she was bigger, stronger and smarter than them. And I wasn't alone. From about the age of twelve I made friends with lots of other kids like me. Kids who didn't fit, who were from broken homes, who were looking for escape. And here's the cruncher: in 1995, in Auckland, having sex at twelve and thirteen years old was relatively common among the kids I knew. And that was before social media. Before every teenager had a Facebook account and a smartphone.

Now I'm a mother, and the thought of my daughter having sex in the next ten years absolutely sickens me. But I'm also a realist and I know I have to prepare her for the predators out there. And the hardest part of that will be telling her that some of those predators may be the boys that she likes. Boys on Facebook. Boys from school. The other thing I have to tell her is that sometimes girls can be predators. And here I'm referring to 'groomers'. I knew a groomer once, although we didn't call her that. We thought she was cool and fun. She was three years older than me and my friends, and she liked hanging out with us. She was tall and broad-shouldered and she liked playing the 'bodyguard' for us smaller-sized girls. She also liked introducing us to older guys. That was her thing. She would introduce us, so she could get 'in' with them. It all seemed pretty innocent back then, but now I can see it for what it was. She was pimping us out and we didn't even know it.

I said this wasn't going to be an easy read. But it's the truth, and it needs to be talked about. How well are we preparing our kids for the predatory environment that is an inevitable part of our society? Are we doing them, or us, any favours by pretending that they are going to save their virginity until they're eighteen or older? Sadly, I don't think so. The more honest we can be with our kids and ourselves the better. So, yes, let's talk about sex. But let's talk about it with honesty.

### 3. A Word From the Margin

It's three in the morning and I have just under three days to go before my second baby's due date. I know, I should be asleep. But as any expectant mum will tell you, in the final few days leading up to a baby's birth, your body clock starts to act up. I think it's part of a weird primal instinct that kicks into gear to 'prepare' you for the inevitable sleepless nights to come. Anyway, I'm up now and after deciding to use this opportunity to catch up on the day's news, I am incensed. Why? Because I've just read an article that outlines the position of the prime minister, John Key, on the widening gap between rich and poor in this country. His position? The gap isn't widening but 'maybe at the margin it has become slightly less unequal'.[*]

In May 2014, the University of Otago released its findings from in-depth analysis of the 2013 census data which showed that 'most Māori and Pacific people still live in socially deprived areas'.[†] Putting two and two together, when the PM refers to 'the margin' he is (whether intentionally or not) referring to most Māori and Pacific people.

As a Pacific woman who is committed to making a contribution to turning this situation around, you can imagine

---

[*]  Niko Kloeten and Josh Fagan, 'PM John Key defends equality after protest', Stuff, 16 May 2014 (www.stuff.co.nz/national/politics/10052733/PM-John-Key-defends-equality-after-rowdy-protest).

[†]  Harkanwal Singh, 'Where are New Zealand's Most Deprived Areas?', *New Zealand Herald*, 13 May 2014.

that this reference to 'the margin' – who collectively happen to make up almost one-fifth of New Zealand's population AND in the case of Māori are tangata whenua – has really pissed me off. He may as well just come out and say it how it is: we are marginalised in this country. So if he knows this, and gives a damn, what is his government doing about it? It's time to stop ignoring what's very clear: the gap is widening and we need to do more before an acutely apparent situation becomes the entrenched status quo. At a guess (taking into account that Māori and Pacific birth rates are almost double the national average) we've got about 25 years, one generation, to turn things around. So we need visionary leaders, with magnanimity, who are willing to work with these communities to make that happen. Not people who draw up imaginary margins in their minds to conveniently ring-fence what is, for many of us, an everyday reality.

## 4. Reflections on Racism and Real Estate (Following an Evening in Ponsonby)

A few months ago I was sitting outside my aunty's house on Pompallier Terrace in Ponsonby, enjoying a glass of wine with a friend. It was one of those memorable late nights where a bunch of us had gone out on Ponsonby Road, had a good time and then headed home to Aunty Teri's place for a snooze before getting picked up in the morning. It's a kind of tradition, and seeing Aunty Teri in the morning always makes it worth it. She gives us all big hugs and welcomes everyone into her home with love.

In the wee hours of that morning, a group of early-twenty-somethings walked past, and we struck up a conversation with them. One of them mentioned that he lived across the road. I asked him which house he lived in and he pointed to a house opposite Aunty Teri's. It happened to be two doors down from the house across the road being sold. He noted the 'for sale' sign. In response, I said it was a shame that the family was selling – they were a lovely Sāmoan family who had lived there for a long time.

The young man said, 'You must be mistaken. If they're Sāmoans they must be renting that house.' 'Excuse me?' I said, hoping that maybe I had misheard him. But he continued prattling on about how there was no way a Sāmoan family 'could afford to live in Ponsonby'.

Trying to be somewhat constructive – even at two in the morning – I took a deep breath. 'Well, actually, no. I know for a fact that family owns that house. Of course, you know that Pacific Island families have lived in Ponsonby and Grey Lynn for over fifty years now, right?' As it turned out, he didn't. So I gave him a brief rundown of local history and suggested he read a few books. Undeterred, he responded that the history didn't matter anyway because 'most of them had moved out to South Auckland now'.

My blood was boiling. I stood up and said to the young man that his attitude was discriminatory and racist. How would he like it, I asked, if I made broad generalisations about whether his ethnic group could or couldn't afford to live in Ponsonby? (I thought at that point he might back down: his friends were looking pretty uncomfortable, and my friend was telling me to calm down).

And then he went for the bull's-eye: 'Why would you care anyway? You're not Sāmoan.'

'Actually,' I said, 'I am Sāmoan, and how dare you make any assumptions about me or my family. This is my aunty's house and she's lived here for almost fifty years.' Very quickly, he and his friends left. Lucky he did too, because I might have thrown something at him if my friend hadn't stopped me. All I had to hand was a shoe, but that would have done.

This isn't the first time someone (non-Pacific) has made discriminatory comments that I've then torn apart. Would he have said those things to my face if I 'looked' more Pacific, if I had darker skin? Based on his reaction after I mentioned the fact, I don't think so.

In the feke that is Auckland (to borrow poet Karlo Mila's brilliant metaphor for this 'octopus of a city') I think we need to be ever-conscious about getting out and learning about our communities. Find out who our neighbours are and the local history of the place. Talking and writing about racism and discrimination, as and when (because in my experience it's not a matter of 'if') we confront it, is an important part of putting those attitudes in their place. As a cultural diplomat, I'd recommend trying those approaches first, but I guess there's always the last-ditch option – we can choose to throw a shoe at the person and tell them to get off our porch.

### 5. Mouths Wide Shut

My husband easily fits the *Crimewatch* stereotype. He is Polynesian, tall, solid, wears hoodies and ripped jeans, has multiple tattoos and long hair . . . the list goes on. He is also university educated, respectful and kind. A few years ago I dragged him along to a writers' event at a library. He wasn't overly keen but agreed to come along to support me. When we arrived, he walked over to the librarian to ask whether he could use the bathroom. She told him they did not have a bathroom, so he would have to walk a block down the road to use the public toilets at the local soccer field. Busting to go, he explained that he was with the writers' group and pleaded to use the bathroom in the library. The woman said, 'No, the library's bathroom isn't available tonight,' and directed him outside. Five minutes later, that same person stood up in front of the other twenty or so guests (all fair-skinned) and said that if anyone needed to use the bathroom, it was just around the corner to the left, in the library.

At the time, the situation seemed clear cut. My husband was, at a glance, the only person of colour in the room. He was the only person sent outside to use the toilet. Surely this woman's response was based on ingrained racial preju-dice. The problem was, how could we prove it? We didn't have any hard evidence, only his word against hers, which didn't seem like enough to take things further. At the time we also lacked the financial means to seek legal advice. So we did what a lot of New Zealanders do when confronted with situations like this. Nothing.

Making a decision to speak out against racism is tough. There are personal risks, including losing a job, being publicly humiliated and ostracised by peers. But keeping silent means those same realities are borne by the victims of discrimination every day. This issue is not going to go away. We all have to make the call: how long will we keep our mouths wide shut?

## José Barbosa
# My Swim with Kim

'Look, you need to have some fucking balls.'

There may have been spittle landing on my chin as these words escaped my mouth. I may have immediately followed through with a barely stifled beer burp, the kind that filled my nose with the smell of hops and armpits. I may have farted ever so softly, punctuating 'balls' with a puff of camembert-laced bum gust. But what cannot be disputed is that the very large German man seated next to me on the opulent sofa looked irritated. Ben leaned into view from behind our Teutonic host with a look on his face you could only translate as 'What the fuck, bro?'

I had just told Kim Dotcom his music video was shithouse.

Only four hours earlier I had been in a salt-water pool (38 degrees Celsius) cracking wise with some affable European millionaires and making a knob out of myself on Twitter. This is what happened.

∗

On the afternoon of 24 June 2012 I was at the computer doing some work when indicted internet entrepreneur, former hacker and hot-tub enthusiast Kim Dotcom tweeted a photo of a happy-looking man on a Segway flanked by two others

First published in *The Pantograph Punch*, 8 August 2012 (http://pantograph-punch.com/my-swim-with-kim/).

on quad bikes, with the caption: 'My alleged co-conspirators enjoying a wonderfully sunny Sunday at the Mansion.'

You can think what you like about Dotcom, but in his artisanal construction of novelty photos – and cheerful sharing of them on social media – one finds a creative mind forever searching for scenarios that best prove how empty life was before shotguns and bubble bath.

My friend Ben Gracewood, the man infamous for ditching a recurring high-profile guest spot on breakfast television because the host was a bit of a dick, responded: 'Do you guys just drive around in modified electric vehicles and pose for photos? I could live like that.' Kim's reply – 'Come over!' – was to have profound consequences for my goal of getting some work done that afternoon.

As we travelled north to Coatesville in Ben's cosy Subaru, we couldn't help but giggle at the thought of the forthcoming escapades. Would Kim and the boys whip out crossbows and hunt us for sport, à la the 1994 Ice-T vehicle *Surviving the Game*? What a hoot that would be, we laughed. Suddenly Ben turned serious. 'Oh my God,' he said, 'what if they pull out a whole bunch of cocaine and some prostitutes turn up?' This seemed a more likely scenario and one we hadn't considered. 'That would be awkward,' I agreed, particularly as cocaine usually doesn't come in bunches. We concluded that if indeed the white lady was present in both human and alkaloid form we'd leave inconspicuously, possibly through a bathroom window.

At the gatehouse a slightly nervous young guy (cocaine shakes?!) dressed in black took our details and, after talking to someone on a phone, opened the solid-looking doors into Germanic Park. Ben piloted the Subaru up the winding driveway to the mansion, and as a guard directed him into a parking space in front of a huge garage, two life-sized giraffe statues appeared on the hill: 'Welcome to the House that Overpriced Christmas Hampers Built,' they seemed to say.

We were ushered through the house to the pool where we finally met our hosts, Kim Dotcom, Finn Batato, Mathias Ortmann and Bram van der Kolk. As we splashed around in the pool we feverishly tweeted more novelty photos. They mostly showed a group of pleased-looking men holding drinks in a pool. I must point out that due to water refraction my moobs appear twice as pillowy in the photos as they are in the flesh.

As the afternoon slowly turned into the evening, #swimatkims started to trend on Twitter; a fact our hosts found quite amusing. They talked briefly about the notorious raid on the mansion; Finn Batato described having a gun pointed at him. They all argued they'd done nothing wrong. Kim repeated what he'd told John Campbell on the 1 March 2012 broadcast of *Campbell Live*: that American law, specifically the Digital Millennium Copyright Act (DMCA), protected Megaupload from third-party breaches of copyright. (That episode was also notable for the way Campbell belted out his description of cloud storage: 'Giant exchange system in the sky!')

At that point, Dotcom's lawyers were arguing in the High Court that the search warrant was illegal because it was overly broad. Four days after our pool party, Justice Helen Winkelmann would rule in their favour. The search warrant was invalid, she said, and it was illegal for the FBI to take copies of Dotcom's hard drives back with them to the United States. Even before the Winkelmann ruling, serious questions were being asked about due process. Suffice it to say that if the police ploughing over the law to satisfy the needs of a foreign power doesn't concern you, congratulations! You get to play outside with this old tyre in a sludge pool made from John Key's discarded facial masks.

Presuming Kim and his team ever get extradited to the States, his defence will be that Megaupload fits the 'safe harbour' provisions of the DMCA. In other words, if web companies quickly take down copyright-infringing material when alerted by the copyright holders, they can't be held liable for how third parties are using their services. People most often use YouTube as an example: can Google really be held accountable, they ask, for people sticking their *Murder She Wrote* tributes on YouTube? This is exactly what Google argued in 2007 when the mass-media giant Viacom filed a lawsuit seeking over $1 billion dollars in compensation for copyright infringement. A 2010 summary judgment was made in Google's favour, and that's undoubtedly the precedent Team Dotcom's lawyer Ira Rothken will refer to if they end up in US court.

The US Department of Justice is arguing that the indicted parties conspired to facilitate copyright infringement by offering financial incentives to users who uploaded popular content. This practice, and variations on it, is standard for cyberlocker sites like Megaupload. But the DoJ alleges the accused were not distant service providers, dutifully removing content when asked; rather, they were right in there, hands-on, driving traffic to Megaupload by actively encouraging illegal sharing. (In the meantime, the road to that end game has taken so many twists and turns it's become a plot-development bird's nest worthy of George R. R. Martin. In early 2014, the New Zealand Court of Appeal overturned Judge Winkelmann's ruling on the mansion raid.)

I was starting to appreciate the surreal nature of my situation. Here I was with a group of people who'd found themselves at the centre of a legal, technological and cultural argument that would most likely change our definition of property and public culture. And we were drinking beer (apart from Kim: he doesn't drink) and tweeting pictures of ourselves eating cupcakes in a pool. These were the same pictures the *New Zealand Herald* would plaster over the cover and page two the next day, along with a story about a *Reader's Digest* survey claiming Richie McCaw was the most trustworthy person in New Zealand. Also covered in the same issue was that week's pending vote in Parliament on the partial sale of state assets: it made page four.

Kim was friendly, everything you'd expect of a fun-loving German playboy. 'Before you leave,' he grinned, 'you must see my new video.' I didn't see any problem with that. He enthusiastically described his new venture Megabox, a site which would, as he described to the file-sharing website Torrentfreak, 'allow artists to sell their creations direct to consumers,' allowing them to keep 90 per cent of their earnings. Central to this was Megakey, a program that users would download to their computers. Megakey, he told us, would substitute advertising on third-party websites with its own. The revenue collected would go to pay artists who stored their music on Megabox for free. Depending on your view, this either sounds like a new model for an old system that was failing rather spectacularly, or a gangland-style execution of traditional media.

I suggested that people would accuse him of stealing their business. At that point the cherubic face of our host dropped. He grumbled something about people being able to opt out and then floated to the other side of the pool. A few minutes later he was back, conceding that I had simply told him what I thought the main criticism would be. 'And I knew that anyway,' he sniffed, staring into the distance like a man harassed by the snapping maw of smaller minds burdened by trifling matters such as intellectual property and creative sovereignty.

They had nice things to say about *Media7*, the former television show I worked on. Kim said the show had the most balanced analysis in the aftermath of their arrest. Presumably unaware of any irony, he lamented the state of journalism and the way their case had been covered. Much later, while relaxing by the fireplace in the pool house, I asked Bram if he agreed that the creation of the internet and the web led to audiences migrating away from traditional media and if this, in turn, had decimated advertising revenue. 'Of course you guys aren't to blame,' I said, 'but you're part of that world. What if the old system was actually the best business model for creating the largest amount of quality journalism?'

Bram looked at me for a moment. 'Some things always lose out when better things come along,' he said.

I think at this point it's fair to say that I'd been enjoying myself. Kim and his wife Mona were excellent hosts, everyone seemed genuinely warm and I was on fire. Sample exchange:

Bram: 'Hey, you look like someone famous. You look like –'

Me: 'Brad Pitt!'

Everyone: Laughter

Boy, I was slaying.

I was also quite pissed. I'd cracked through the beer Ben and I had brought along and was making decent headway through the house reserves. By the time Kim suggested Ben and I have a look at his new music video, I'd been weighing up the chances of finding a long forgotten wing of the mansion and curling up for forty winks in a discarded Chrisco hamper display.

We followed Kim past the kitchen with the huge fish tank filled with nearly sixty tropical fish, then through room after room until we found ourselves sitting in front of a flat-screen television so big it could've doubled as a shelterbelt. Kim pressed play and we watched the video for 'Hey Mr President', an anthem for internet freedom disguised as mid-nineties chart bait. Sample lyric: 'We must expose / the people who chose / to turn innovation into crime.' The video features a confusing reference to Martin Luther King, and people protesting in the street dressed in the famous Guy Fawkes masks as appropriated by the Scientology-griefers, Anonymous. But no images of Barack Obama himself, which struck me as a little odd.

'Well,' said Kim 'I think people will know who we're talking about.'

Which, of course, is a reasonable thing to say, but right then and there I wasn't really doing reasonable. 'If you say "Mr President", show the President!'

Kim turned to the table behind us where the other three accused and their wives and partners had silently assembled. 'What do you think?' he asked. The sentiment from the room was clear. They were against rocking the boat with Obama too much. And, more importantly, they were against disagreeing with Kim.

It was then that I questioned the composition of Dotcom's genitalia. The room filled with the sound of blood vessels popping as everyone held their breath. Then I really got going: 'I think you should go and interview Alan Moore, who wrote the book those Guy Fawkes masks came from, because, y'know, it makes it legitimate I mean I think it's perfectly fine and all but oh what we're going oh OKAY NICE MEETING YOU.'

We rounded up our togs and bits and pieces and walked back out the main door, past the dinner table. Kim was sitting at it, looking like someone had just told him he had no balls. 'THANKS FOR THE SWIM BYE!'

Back in the Subaru, Ben swore he'd been leaving anyway.

It's all good, he assured me. Funny, even. But no, we can't stop at Burger King. Bastard.

I stumbled through my front door and down to the bedroom where my partner was reading in bed. Did I have a good time, she asked? YEP GREAT I HAD A SWIM. That's nice, she said, come to bed – knowing full well I'd be asleep as soon as my head touched the pillow, restoring the quiet.

In no state to bother with official sleeping attire, I dropped my trousers. But something was not quite right. My girlfriend peered over her book. 'What's wrong?'

I lifted my T-shirt up and looked down. Where there should have been cotton boxers, there was only pool-wrinkled flesh constricting in the chill of the uninsulated room. I had left my undies at Kim Dotcom's.

# Ashleigh Young
## Small Revolutions,
## or: On My Bike in London

### I.

Yesterday I saw a man striding along Kennington Road in normal civilian clothing, except for the motorcycle helmet he was wearing. Out of curiosity I looked around for his motorbike. No sign of it anywhere. Immediately the man seemed insane. Why is it that as soon as you step away from the thing for which a helmet is required, you look ridiculous? (I'm reminded of my great-uncle James – renowned for falling off a succession of scooters – who is known to have worn his full-face motorcycle helmet when at the movies. I think this was to protect himself from Jaffas launched by kids in the rows behind him, or maybe it was to create a sense of total head-cushioned seclusion. I'll never know. Possible clue: he always held his head at an angle in photos.) I wish it were more socially acceptable to wear a helmet around so that you didn't have to go to the trouble of putting it on and taking it off when you got on/off your bike. (Could it be that this is what Uncle James was protesting?)

Maybe the reason it looks funny to wear a helmet sans vehicle or sportsfield is that it's become kind of unusual to wear a hat, except for a beanie in winter, or if you're in uniform or religious dress or are going to a party. The western world lives

Based on a selection of posts first published on Ashleigh's blog Eyelash Roaming, 2011 and 2012 (eyelashroaming.com).

in a largely hatless age. So to wear non-contextual headgear reads as some kind of affectation. An extreme example: a friend recalls seeing a woman walking along wearing a phone strapped around her head with a scarf. Like a bandage, wrapped around her head, securing the phone in place.

It's been claimed that forcing people to wear helmets, as is the case in New Zealand where it's the law, will put them off cycling. I guess because they fear looking silly. Helmet wearing has always been controversial among cyclists, and now another study has found that cycle helmets don't offer much protection at all against head injuries.* I haven't made up my mind on this one. The problem is I'm too suggestible. 'Oh, so the no-helmet brigade is anti-capitalist nonsense and if you hit me over the head with a baseball bat, would I rather have a helmet on or off? Well, then . . .' 'Oh, so my helmet could leave me *worse off* than not wearing one in some situations and helmets are a sign of a failed cycle culture? Well, then . . .' The problem is also instinct: my instinct to wear a helmet is as strong as my instinct to wear underwear. It was embedded in early childhood. I can't see much further beyond the – some would say delusional – sense of safety that a helmet gives me, and the stark vulnerability I feel if I'm not wearing one.

I've noticed something interesting, though: whenever I wear a pink helmet, most drivers give me more space when they overtake. But when I wear my ordinary old sporty black one, I get a lot more punishment passes. The 'punishment pass' is a move that my brother Neil, also a keen London cyclist, describes as being 'strafed by a passing car or

---

* Jonathon Harker, 'Cycle helmets offer little protection against head injuries', *BikeBiz*, 9 March 2012 (www.bikebiz.com/news/read/cycle-helmets-offer-little-protection-against-head-injuries).

motorbike while on a bike: the sudden onrush of terror as a vehicle slices past mere centimetres from your body, engine revving, driver gesticulating and/or yelling abuse, followed by the sense of outrage, heightened by the fact that you have no recourse in such situations'.* Something about the appearance of the pink helmet seems to invite a more gentle response from the driver. He or she must make a snap judgement about the kind of cyclist you are, and that reaction is: 'Pink: let her live.' This makes me uncomfortable. But not uncomfortable enough to stop wearing the pink helmet as a safety strategy.

## 2.

Nothing makes me feel less special than riding my bike to work in the mornings. In a spidery mass of commuting cyclists, you're just one more pair of legs to get in the way of someone else's. Because it's spring, the bike lanes have been seething. As soon as blossom fills the trees, bikes fill the bike lanes, bugs fill the cyclists' mouths, and the cyclists sing, or they whistle. I don't like it when people sing as they cycle. Whistling is even worse. There's something self-congratulatory about that jollity. 'Look at me,' the singer/whistler is saying. 'I'm carefree and joyous as I ride my bicycle.' Suddenly everyone else seems conspicuously silent – joyless, even. Even if the singer/whistler noticed other cyclists glaring, it wouldn't upset them. Because they are so joyous. I'm all for joie de vivre, but it's not a competition.

The thing is, I find it difficult to entertain any smuggery about cycling. I can't congratulate myself on being 'one less car' or 'running on fat, not money'. And I can't wholeheartedly

---

\* Neil Young, 'So That's What That Is', Wolfie Stories, 21 January 2012 (https://wolfiestories.wordpress.com/2012/01/23/so-thats-what-that-is/).

believe, as the cycle activism group Zero Per Gallon argues, that cycling is like

> eating a super-duper delicious burrito every day with guaca-
> mole and cheese and sauce on top at the most fabulous taqueria
> mankind has ever seen, and discovering that it makes your butt
> look good AND it makes you feel good AND it's extending
> your life AND it's saving you money. Oh, yeah – and it's also
> helping solve huge international crises, like healthcare and global
> warming and energy.*

Of course cycling is broadly preferable to other forms of transport. On a good day I love cycling and feel proud of it. The benefits for me are mostly anti-social ones: the inde-pendence, the avoidance of public transport and the exercise. But it's not a silver bullet. It doesn't make you Captain Planet, or even a fine upstanding citizen.

I wish it did, but you can ride a bike and also be a bastard. You can run red lights at such speed that you almost take out parents with toddlers crossing at the green man. You can cycle 100 miles a day and yet contribute to any number of international crises. I'll concede that cycling saves me money (but even on that front, considering the thefts and repairs and insurance I've paid for, the margins are slim). Whether it makes my bum look any better is still up for debate but evidence tells me let's not talk about it. And my secret cycling shame is this: sometimes, *cycling does not make me feel good*. On a bad day it makes me feel like rubbish. It fills me with ill-feeling for my fellow man.

---

* Zero Per Gallon, 'About' (www.zeropergallon.com/about/).

3.

Riding home after work on a cold Wednesday I pulled up behind a big red bus at an intersection on Brixton Road. It was dark, and I could see parts of my reflection in the bus. I have two white lights on the front of my bike; one light is flashing and the other is steady. I saw the reflection of the two lights. The lights looked like eyes in a face, looking straight into me, half glaring, half winking. I saw that face as the face of death.

In Wellington, I used to imagine picturesque, almost delicate deaths. I died by being blown by the wind into the harbour; or my brakes failed when I went down an 80-degree-angled hill. My imagined deaths are very different over here. In a roundabout snarling with buses and cabs, I find myself encircled by alternate universes in which I'm getting killed in all sorts of ways. Suddenly a lorry is whomping overheard, or I'm being squeezed to death between buses, or the shape of my body is imprinted on the flung-open door of a car. I'm not sure if I'm really afraid: I think it's that I have become habitually alert to the fact of possible death. The alertness has become hyperactive caution. *What might happen* has become too vivid.

At time of writing, sixteen cyclists have been killed in London in 2011, twelve of them by heavy goods vehicles, and one on the road where I work. I have passed a couple of crash sites: the telltale sign of an ambulance and a discarded bicycle with an orange cone next to it. *The orange cone.*

One day, a few weeks ago, my bike was at the mechanic, so I walked down to the Underground. I was actually looking forward to taking the Tube; it would be nice to sit down and read the paper, and just be motionless, not thinking of death. The Tube is great for looking at things, too, like people's shoes, and the books they're reading. But there were severe delays that morning. We were sitting in the carriage for ages, not moving. Then the announcement came: 'There is a body on the tracks.'

Everyone in the carriage groaned. My brother Neil calls this 'the existential groan'.

Death in the Underground is tragic and horrible, and what makes it even more tragic and horrible is that it's so routine. One can use it as a legitimate excuse for being late to work, and this excuse will be shrugged off by one's boss. I wonder if the fact that these tragedies are so routine, often so banal, makes it hard for us to be constructively aware of them. By constructive, I mean an awareness that compels us to live more fully. I mean the falling-away of unimportant things, as Steve Jobs explained in his 2005 commencement address at Stanford: 'Remembering that I'll be dead soon is the most important tool I've ever encountered to help me make the big choices in life. Because almost everything – all external expectations, all pride, all fear of embarrassment or failure – these things just fall away in the face of death, leaving only what is truly important.'

However, the awareness of death that I have been experiencing is not constructive, but hyper. This is like a thin gauze of morbidity over my eyes, darkening everything I see. Traffic lights in disrepair have bags thrown over their heads, tied around their necks. The ungreased chains of advancing cyclists squeak like rats. The front of each bus seems poised to become a gaping maw.

Yesterday I was talking about this with Neil. He described being run off the road by a speeding car whose driver was talking on a phone. 'I heard myself let out a bellow of utter fear,' he said, 'and I realised it was the death fear.' (Viral video idea: take field recordings of cyclists' bellows of death fear and then present them in some kind of humorous yet hard-hitting cycle awareness campaign, not unlike the New Yorker cyclist Casey Neistat who documented himself crashing into various obstacles in official bike lanes, including a parked police car.)

Perhaps my brother and I, and anyone whose daily commute has filled them with despair, need to relearn how to momentarily suspend our belief in death. Most of us do this automatically. Why else would we travel in cabooses 200 feet underground, practically in moving graves? Why else would we leave our houses?

The accepted wisdom for London cyclists is to ride as though everybody is trying to kill you. (As Homer Simpson says, peering into Bart's face: 'People die all the time, just like that. Why, you could wake up dead tomorrow! . . . Well, good night.') I'm all for defensive cycling. But I'm not sure that maintaining a they're-trying-to-kill-you philosophy will help you feel good about being alive. We soon become pickled in our own rancid fear and loathing of other road users, and it is not then easy to break out of that mindset. And as cyclists, we are already more present in the 'fearscape' of the city than drivers, as Lancaster cyclist Dave Horton puts it in a fine piece from his blog Thinking About Cycling:

> The city is full of fear, which is partly why and partly because people move in cars. Increasing car use can be seen as a retreat from the 'public' world of the city, a means of cocooning oneself and one's family from 'the outside', from fear of traffic but also from dangerous places and people. Cycling puts the person back into this fearscape in a much less mediated way.[*]

---

[*]    Dave Horton, 'Fear of Cycling', Thinking About Cycling (http://thinkingaboutcycling.com/article-fear-of-cycling/).

One strategy I've been trying out when I ride, purely to quell my morbid imaginings, is to construct an imaginary cocoon of safety. I do this by thinking of cars and buses as my friends. In this vision, I'm a suckerfish on the backs of the big friendly giants of the sea: the whales and dolphins. (Bear with me here.) I came up with this when I had the realisation, while riding alongside a bus, that the bus was shielding me from other traffic. It was also stopping pedestrians from darting out in front of me, because pedestrians are much more likely to wait for a bus to pass than they are for a bike.

This strategy completely upends my usual way of thinking about traffic. It is clearly counter-intuitive, possibly foolish. But it momentarily calms my hyper-awareness of death and puts me back in the landscape as opposed to the fearscape.

Sometimes, when a car is cruising along beside me, I think how much like old friends we are – just rolling along together, two benign species. At the end of the road, well, we're both glad to be at the end of the road. We park our bikes or our cars and go into our houses and make ourselves dinner.

## 4.

On my ride to work, there's one intersection where I often pass an old man with a wiry moustache walking his dog. The man is usually muttering and whistling loudly – he's always making some kind of noise. He seems unhinged in an amiable sort of way. Passersby ignore him and I've never seen him hassle anyone. But a few times lately, he's been in a bad mood. He's ranting and raving at his dog, as if his dog has done something to enrage him, as if the dog were a parking warden trying to ticket him or a council worker who refuses to take his rubbish bags away. This isn't just a straight scolding or dressing down – this is a serious disagreement, a heated argument about why the man is in the right and the dog is in the wrong. The man is really yelling, waving his hands around. Meanwhile the poor dog just doesn't know what to do. It slinks along beside him looking down at the footpath, defeated, oppressed by his owner who has all this language. It looks like an old dog, because it doesn't trot along like healthy dogs do – instead it walks, one leg at a time.

When I came across this scene the other day I was reminded of that old chestnut 'the black dog' – our preferred metaphor for depression. It hounds us, it slavers all over us and howls at night. But I wondered if a more appropriate metaphor for depression is the *owner* of the dog. In this case, you yourself are the dog. Your owner is bigger and seems more powerful than you and he is full of this impenetrable language. And he's got you on a leash and has trained you to think he's in charge, and you're stuck with him.

Frankly, this hasn't been a good week for the bike. I've been reminded too many times of all the things that grate me about cycling, the things that shred my mood into slivers of rage and wretchedness.

Today I was lashed in the face by a springing bungee while trying to tie my bag to my rack. Then I rode through a pothole so huge and jagged that my carefully assembled bag-contraption bounced off and fell on the road. Black cabs beeped. Cars cut me up. (In New Zealand I'd say 'cut me off' but 'cut me up' is so much more apt – picture a giant pair of scissors snipping your pathway into bits.) A man shouted, 'It's a red light, *red light*, fucken tosser cyclists,' while I was waiting patiently at the red light. A little old man in a suit, riding a Boris Bike, crept up on my inside, nearly causing us to clump together. A motorbike roared past inches from my elbow. A kid on a bus did the fingers at me. My legs ache. My knee clicks so badly

I sound like a broken cassette tape. Another cyclist crashed into a pedestrian talking on her cellphone as she crossed the road. Running late for an appointment (with a chiropractor, because my neck is bung from looking over my shoulder all the time while riding), I couldn't find anywhere to tether my bike, and when I finally did, my lock wouldn't fit the pole. So I was really late for my appointment, and when I got into the room, my back took this as a signal that it could now gush with post-ride sweat.

Another challenge to my enthusiasm for the bike is that fact that the bike, along with the hoodie, has become a symbol of the London riots of August 2011. Bikes gave rioters the agility and speed to carry out crimes then flee, to quickly pass messages and loot from one to another, to congregate then scatter in seconds. The bicycle itself became highly coveted loot: along with Micycle, branches of Evans in Chalk Farm and Clapham were ransacked, and Halfords in Brixton. There were reports of people being mugged for their bikes in London Fields, and of looters in Clapham using Boris Bikes, the most humble, benign bikes ever, as getaway vehicles.

Today, just as I was beginning to sob into the wind and incoming rain, I realised I was seeing these things as a personal affront. Enthusiasm for cycling is like a tyre: ignore it, and sooner or later it will deflate and your ride will become heavier, every pedal-stroke a drag. Thus, day in, day out, cycling becomes a misery.

Obviously I needed to a) harden up, and b) remind myself why I do this. As I slogged up Tulse Hill, holding up yet another bus, I tried to identify reasons for continuing to cycle. I thought about the usual suspects, such as the childlike sense of freedom, the wind in one's hair/helmet, the ringing bell, not having to take the Tube, the negligible carbon footprint. These are fine, noble reasons. But in the end, most of my reasons for cycling are selfish and shallow, and I hold them dear.

1. A tailwind.
2. Being passed by someone furiously pedalling on a tiny-wheeled Brompton folding bike, because this means that it's all over and I may as well just give up and go at my own pace.
3. Being nearly hit by a pigeon, and feeling an intense buzz of relief at not being hit. (The same goes for being nearly hit by cars, buses, motorbikes and other cyclists.)
4. Riding over Waterloo Bridge and seeing the giant straw sculpture of the sad *Urban Fox* hunkered outside the Hayward Gallery.
5. A friendly driver who flashes their lights to tell you to go first. Then they give you a wave and a nod when you let them go first.
6. A pedestrian who gives you a grin when you stop at a zebra crossing, as if a cyclist stopping at a pedestrian crossing is a sign that not all people are bad, really.
7. Beer tastes better.
8. Coffee tastes better.
9. Food tastes better.
10. Cycling through delicious food smells.
11. Cycling past cafés and pubs and thinking, Oooh, that looks nice. And occasionally stopping and tethering my bike to a pole outside.
12. Buying or perusing bike-related items. A bottle cage, night lights, mudguards, bells. Bells, but not whistles.
13. Ogling other people's fancy bikes, or ogling the rider while pretending to ogle the bike.
14. Reading bicycle blogs and commentary and disagreeing

with people and getting worked up. The cyclist-blogger community is something for me to engage in and have strong opinions about. There are few areas in which I can justifiably do this.

15. My ridiculous pink helmet, and choosing not to wear it some days.
16. Freshly pumped tyres and a newly sealed road.
17. The grimace of camaraderie with fellow cyclists when a driver/pedestrian/other cyclist does something life-threatening and gets away with it.
18. Sometimes seeing a cyclist carrying a little dog in a special backpack.
19. When it stops drizzling and the sun comes out.
20. Feeling like part of a movement that's much bigger than me, something that will inevitably change the shape of our towns and cities.
21. Riding past people waiting at bus stops; when they hold up their hands to hail the bus, it's like they're angling for a high-five from me.
22. A post-ride shower and huge cup of strong Assam tea.

I suppose that when you're beginning to think you might hate doing something, the best course of action is to ask yourself why you do it. This goes for anything. It could be, in fact, that you don't hate it, only that you've become intoxicated by the anger and disappointment at the bad things that happen along your way, an intoxication which steadily distorts your view. I like to hope that anger and disappointment are just part of the gauntlet of feelings we must simply ride through. It's possible to arrive at your destination feeling pleased with yourself despite this gauntlet, or at the very least, relieved that it's behind you and that maybe you are the tougher for it.

## Paul Ewen
# The King and I

*Yes, he emphasised, a little country; and with inhabitants so much limited in number it was unlikely you would even hear them rattle on any occasion when the Almighty took it into his head to shake their little country . . .* – Frank Sargeson

New Zealand is blessed with a great deal of space. This makes it a big drawcard for overseas visitors, a fact not lost on the tourism industry, which commissions epic landscape photographs, usually barren and sparse, depicting vast mountain ranges, the purest lakes and fiords, untouched rolling countryside and large majestic pools of bubbling mud. You could be forgiven for thinking that no people actually live there.

As a New Zealander, I have managed to see a great deal of my country, much of it through the window of my mate's brown Cortina. In its day, Steve's Cortina transported the pair of us on a series of epic trips around the South and North islands. Steve always drove (apart from one late-night incident in Cromwell when I mounted the footpath), and he always insisted the Cortina was in fact copper, not brown. At every new town we visited, a felt pennant was added to the car aerial, and these flags rippled in the southern-hemisphere winds, most being reduced to tufty dags by the end of each given trip.

First published under the title 'Space' in *Five Dials*, no. 32, 1 June 2014 (http://fivedials.com/fivedials).

To occupy ourselves while travelling through the (undeniably magnificent) landscape, we would sometimes play car
cricket, scoring runs based on the plenitude of oncoming
traffic. An approaching car, for instance, would be one run,
a motorbike two, and a truck four, but a passing campervan
meant the 'batsman' was out. Occasionally, driving in particularly sparse countryside, such as the west coast of the
South Island, we would wait bloody ages to score a single run.
Some years later, I found myself living in Ho Chi Minh City,
Vietnam, and on the one occasion when I attempted to play
car cricket, I scored about a million runs purely in motorbike
traffic before I had to pull over, cross-eyed.

One of my theories about why there's so much space in
New Zealand springs from the fact that so many of us are
out of the country on any given day. I once read that, after
Germany, New Zealand has the most nationals, per head
of population, living or travelling abroad at any one time.
(A fair counter to my argument, however, may be that most
of the space New Zealanders leave behind is filled, in turn,
with German tourists.) Despite having loads of space at
home, New Zealanders love to spend time in places where
there isn't much space at all. Like aeroplanes. With backpacks
crammed full of undies, T-shirts and woollen socks, they blast
off, funded by student loans, attempting to bridge the vast
gap between their country and the rest of the world. One of
the furthest possible destinations, and also one of the most
popular, is England, some 11,000 miles away. Many English
people claim New Zealand is just like England was fifty years
ago, while most New Zealanders who travel to England believe
its Underground system is just like it was a hundred years ago.

A few years back, Steve and I, both residing in London, flew
home to New Zealand for a funeral. It takes twenty-four hours

to fly from London to New Zealand, which is a very long way to go just for a church service, particularly if you need to return in a matter of days, like I did. There's also the time difference to consider. New Zealand is twelve hours ahead of the United Kingdom (or thirteen hours, depending on daylight savings), so when you fly back to England you lose half a day of your life. Steve, however, had a one-way ticket to New Zealand. He was stretching his legs in the cargo hold. It was his funeral.

Steven MacDonald and I grew up in the small farming town of Ashburton (affectionately referred to as 'Ashvegas'), on the east coast of the South Island. Ashburton has a population of just over 15,000 people and, like many small places in New Zealand, it's a good place to get your driving licence because there's hardly any traffic. If you have a few too many drinks in Ashburton, you can always walk home, because that isn't far away either. The countryside around Ashburton is teeming with livestock, and there's quite an interesting clock feature in the town centre. When we were teenagers, Ashburton was also renowned for its high suicide rate. Livestock, suicides and a clock. It doesn't feature strongly in those tourism ads.

Steve and I became friends at primary school, staying close through high school and sharing a flat together when we moved to Christchurch. We also crossed paths again in Wellington, and when I got married in London, Steve was my best man.

Steve was an exceptional composer, musician and singer. While in the UK he worked as a music teacher, based at a school in Kent. Occasionally I would take the train out to see him, but more often we would meet at a London pub, such as the Champion in Fitzrovia, or the Effra in Brixton.

As a man, Steve took up a lot of space. He was both tall and big, weighing in at an impressive 25 stone. Whenever Steve lowered himself into the Cortina, it would shake like hell. On our first big New Zealand outing, travelling around the South Island, our plan was to camp each night in a two-man tent. On the second night it rained heavily, and Steve awoke in the early hours to find himself in a crater of water his own body had forged. My half was completely dry. We spent the remaining four weeks sleeping, contorted, in the Cortina.

Steve had a lot of mana: in typeface terms, he was something like a 14pt, double-spaced COPPERPLATE GOTHIC LIGHT – but not bold or underlined: he was a very modest bloke. To those who knew him, Steve's physical appearance seemed to fit his exceptional intelligence, humour and principles perfectly. His large head was completely bald, and from his face hung an awe-inspiring thick black beard of Rasputin proportions. He had laughing brown eyes, and his body mass was perfectly suited for heaving with said laughter. Occasionally he would don a look of mock abject fury, and to the uninitiated he must have appeared like the god of thunder himself. With his stature, wisdom and beard, I honestly believe that Steve would have made a truly great king.

Along with two of his closest UK friends and colleagues, I had the task of sorting out Steve's northern-hemisphere life once he'd stopped living. His student accommodation in Kent was nothing more than a tiny room, but he didn't want for much, and he'd been putting money aside to return to South America – a place he'd journeyed to, and became enamoured with, after first leaving home. The week after his death, we went through his quarters, packing things for his family in New Zealand, distributing selected items between his friends and selling the bulk of his possessions to raise money for his school's music department, as per his parents' wishes. Because there were three of us engaged in the task, cataloguing every item into an inventory like documenters at the British Museum, it was a less painful process than I'd expected. What I found more distressing was having to collect Steve's things from London University Hospital, where he was rushed by ambulance on the day he died.

Some of Steve's clothing had been cut end to end with scissors. These items were now bound up in bulky parcels. The contents of his pockets, such as his wallet, keys and loose change, together with his watch and necklace, were tightly pressed in clear plastic bags, like the standard bank-issue type used for coins. His possessions were dispensed from a small room off the hospital's Euston Road entrance, which resembled a downstairs cloakroom in a nightclub. In place of a numbered ticket stub, I presented my New Zealand passport, my arrival having been arranged via an earlier phone call from the New Zealand Embassy. The greying woman who dealt with my collection was probably in her late fifties, and she had a caring and sympathetic manner befitting a funeral director, carefully unwrapping each bag and presenting the contents. In a way, I felt as if I were being handed another man's things on my release from jail, and despite all the items being familiar and recognisable, it felt somehow wrong to claim them.

Frank, one of my fellow documenters at Steve's flat, found me afterwards in the hospital reception with reddened eyes, so we walked around to the nearby Jeremy Bentham pub and drank to our close friend Steve.

The item of Steve's I chose to remember him by was a pounamu necklace, carved in a toki design, representing power, authority and wisdom. I still haven't adjusted the string, so today the greenstone slab hangs down near my belly button. If I'm running it makes a slap, slap noise on my stomach. As a short, thin person, I suppose I am the physical antithesis of Steve. At thirty, I was still getting asked for ID. When someone I know has a baby, I am told it looks, literally, like me. And my wife still laughs when we walk through a particular south London park, ever since I leapt up to grab an overhead tree branch, failed to reach the required height for a sturdy grip and landed flat on my back. Chances are, when I die, they'll put me in an urn, uncremated.

If you can imagine the vast quantities of ocean that stretch between the United Kingdom and New Zealand, you can begin to understand how much I drank on that twenty-four-hour flight back home for Steve's funeral. I had a eulogy to write, and the drinks were free. The problem with drinking too much is that, over time, gaps in your life mysteriously appear. Troublesome voids of space. People talk about writers as vast consumers of alcohol, but I think it's the other way around: drinkers actually become writers in order to document everything they remember before they forget it all.

My suitcase was down with Steve, in the hold. Apart from a few necessities for my brief stay, the case was filled mainly with possessions belonging to him. It was as if he'd packed it himself. Among his things were journals of his South American trips, and also many printed poems, some dating back to our high-school days. There were other items too, such as his watch, his wallet, his bank cards, various souvenirs from his travels, a few reminders of home, and other personal documents and photographs for his family to sift through later. If Steve had known I'd be carting his things back to New Zealand, he probably would have packed something special for the customs officials to discover in my presence. Our border-control laws are renowned for their strict stance when it comes to importing foodstuffs, plant life, wooden items and the like. A deep-fried shoe, say, would have raised some serious questions, and I would have been forced to answer bleary-eyed, melting the officials with my high-octane breath.

Coffins, like beds, are generally made to fit a particular human frame. Steve's casket was a cross between a dining table in a stately home and a Hummer. It was specially made with steel reinforcements, and at the funeral ceremony it had to come through the side doors because it wouldn't fit down the central aisle. Dave, one of the pallbearers, reminded me of a story from our student days. Once, in our dilapidated Christchurch flat, a few of us were teasing Steve about his cooking, and he responded, in mock god-of-thunder fury:

'Right. For that, you bastards can carry my coffin!'

Before the general congregation arrived at the cemetery, Grant, another pallbearer, poured whiskey into the grave, on to Steve's coffin. This was whiskey from a bottle that Steve had left behind for his friends upon departing New Zealand. It was a nice tribute, and after the ceremonies were concluded, a group of us, his old Ashburton mates, got drunk.

Recently, I came across a photo of some astronauts repairing a space-station satellite some 250 miles above New Zealand. You can quite clearly see the Canterbury region, just to the north of Ashburton, where the coastline juts out like a round, knotted piece of wood to form what is known as Banks Peninsula (Te Pātaka o Rākaihautū). The top of the South Island is also visible, and even the distant beginnings of the North Island. The astronauts are not New Zealanders, so they probably don't cherish the view the way I do. They seem very intent on their work, and I imagine they're doing their best not to sneeze into their glass visors. Looking at an image such as that, it's easy to imagine souls ascending through the clouds, up to the heavens; easy to conjure up a romantic vision of Steve's final journey, drifting through the black of space into another realm entirely.

Steve was a big fan of Hunter S. Thompson, and despite the thirty-two-year age gap between the two men, they died within two years of each other. Hunter's cremated ashes were inserted into a fist-shaped cannon that he'd designed with his artist friend Ralph Steadman, and his particles were blasted skywards from a 153-foot tower in Aspen, USA. According to reports I have read, however, Hunter's ashes didn't actually leave the Earth's atmosphere, which thins out some 75 miles above ground level. Steve's final flight may not have had the razzmatazz of a massive fist-cannon launch financed by Johnny Depp. But I take consolation in the epic 11,000-mile journey he took around the world, and the fact that his magnificent person was not compressed to the width and depth of an urn.

Steve died suddenly in Covent Garden, dropping like a stone on a narrow cobbled street called New Row. The emergency services arrived very promptly, but Steve didn't respond to their treatment.

I'm sitting at the end of this cobbled street now, in a pub called the Roundhouse. There's a football match on and it's very crowded. Since the funeral, I haven't managed to get back to Ashburton, so I've yet to drop by on Steve in private and say a few words. I'm glad he wasn't cremated. But with all that space over there, it seems a shame that the only visible reminder of such a larger-than-life fellow is a modest slab of stone poking out of the ground. What Steve needs is some sort of monument, ideally situated next to Ashburton's famous clock. A full-size Cortina statue would be more in keeping, with Steve seated heroically at the wheel. Steve himself would be cast in bronze, but the Cortina would be made out of copper. Real copper. And instead of laying flowers at the wheels, fluffy pennant flags would be added to the aerial. Perhaps I'll write to Johnny Depp and ask for a grant.

I've just come back through the crowded bar with a fresh pint, only to find my table has been commandeered. That's what happens, you see, when there's no one to save your seat.

## Tina Makereti

# He Taonga te Reo: How ngā Kupu Māori Contribute to New Zealand Writing in English

Te reo Māori has always been for me a language in which I expressed that which I could find no words for in English. When I first began to learn the language, this usually meant any expressions of spirituality, and many expressions of culture. It was somehow more acceptable to sing and pray and assert identity in te reo Māori, because it was normal to do those things in that language. I had had a predominantly Pākehā upbringing, which carefully kept a lid on such outward expressions of emotion and spirit.

Still, I was never a very good student of te reo. I didn't manage to become fluent. But I would not be without the small amount of Māori language I am in possession of, especially as a New Zealand writer whose primary medium is English. In 2013, the Nelson Marlborough Institute of Technology invited me to speak at their Cultural Difference Week for their Creative Industries students, who were focusing on te reo so that they could create stop-motion animations about its importance. The students were keen and diverse, with a wide range of questions and understandings about

First given as a talk to the Nelson Marlborough Institute of Technology, April 2013, and published on Tina's website, June 2013 (www.tinamakereti.com/2/post/2013/04/he-taonga-te-reo-how-ng-kupu-mori-contribute-to-nz-writing-in-english.html).

the significance of te reo Māori. I talked to them about how integral te reo is to how I write in English, how integral it is to our identities as New Zealanders, and what a cultural and creative wasteland Aotearoa would be without our indigenous language.

I began by way of a few examples, beginning with a word of some contention . . .

**PĀKEHĀ:** Many of you, as contemporary young New Zealanders, will be completely comfortable with this term, while perhaps your parents or grandparents are not. There are still those who find the term offensive, though I have long wondered why. There are various versions of stories about the origins of the word Pākehā, including that it is an onomatopoeic word for the language Cook and his men spoke when they first arrived, and that its meaning, when broken down, could mean 'those of different breath or language'. One indication that Pākehā is a term still not acceptable for many New Zealanders is that on the recent census form 'New Zealand European' was still the only choice available to white New Zealanders to describe their ethnicity. I am half Pākehā. After I wrote in my iwi, I ticked the 'other' box on my census form and wrote in 'Pākehā'.

The reason for this is that I am proud to be Pākehā, just as I am proud to be Māori. 'New Zealand European' doesn't mean anything to me, and most Pākehā I know are not very European at all. Pākehā only exist in this place, in Aotearoa, and the Pākehā culture was forged on these shores. The name, given to the second people of these lands, says something about relationship to this place and its first people. No one else in the world gets to claim that heritage, no one else gets to have the unique relationship that Pākehā have with Aotearoa and Māori. To be Pākehā is to claim ownership of a position in the most extraordinary country I know. There are responsibilities that come with that position, of course, but I don't want to stray too far from my point. 'New Zealand European' carries none of the rich heritage and history that comes with the word Pākehā. It is part of the story of what makes us, us.

Here are some more terms. My apologies to any speakers of te reo, as I'm going to go over some basic things that are immediately evident when you learn the language, but I'm guessing that many of you haven't. Last week I asked a class I teach at Victoria University how many knew another language. Two out of around eighteen students put their hands up. I was not even asking if they spoke Māori. It's a shame our education system doesn't insist on some level of bilingualism, as is the norm in many overseas countries. Only by learning another language can one gain a clear insight into how a language embodies a different worldview, a whole different way of perceiving and being in the world.

Some basic interpretations:

**HAPŪ:** Hapū means sub-tribe or kinship group (the main form of societal organisation for Māori – villages were centred around hapū). But also, pregnant.

**IWI:** Iwi means tribe – larger kinship group descended from common ancestor. And also, bone; strength.

**WHĀNAU:** Whānau means family – most commonly extended family. It also means to be born, to give birth.

**WHENUA:** Whenua means land. Also, placenta or afterbirth.

Looking at the various meanings of these words, we can learn a great deal about Māori culture. That your iwi is your strength, the structure that holds you upright, as deep and eternal as bones, which remain long after the rest of you has passed, just as your people will. That being hapū, creating new life, is intimately connected to the main group through which Māori society is organised – perhaps that each needs the other. That we are attached to our whenua in much the same way as a babe is attached to her mother's placenta – that it feeds and sustains us.

As a writer, this means that te reo is indispensible to my writing, even in English. There are certain concepts and ideas that can only be expressed in te reo. English approximations cannot give the sense of place or meaning that Māori can.

An example: I recently sent a query to an American agent. She wanted to see the first fifty pages of my novel, which was thrilling, but I had a dilemma. In those first fifty pages were scattered many Māori words. Some could be exchanged for their English equivalent without too much loss of meaning, but most could not. Is *family* really the equivalent of *whānau*? In my first book, I very purpose-fully did not include a glossary (more about that later), and I did not want the American agent to constantly interrupt her reading to look up the Māori words if I did supply one. For a New Zealand reader, I can assume a certain amount of prior knowledge, and make context give meaning for the rest. Here I was less sure.

In the end I compromised. Unless I could be sure the context of the sentence gave the meaning of the word, I used the English translation. But this made the story somehow less than it was. For example, I discovered that I'd used the word 'whare' frequently. Many New Zealanders will know that a

whare is a house. But in this context, the whare were being
built for a summer hunting and gathering expedition. It was
the 1880s, so timber houses also featured, but here the whānau
were travelling to tribal lands and building makeshift whare to
camp in. A New Zealander might easily imagine one – made
from ponga and flax, raupō or driftwood, whatever materials
were available.

For my American reader, I couldn't use the word 'house'
which means a certain solid thing that takes months to
construct and contains many rooms. I couldn't say 'tent',
because obviously that is a cloth construction. In the end I
substituted 'hut'. It was entirely unsatisfactory. Huts bring
to mind buildings in other countries, and colonial descriptions of them. They might be made of mud and cow dung,
be painted bright colours, or be thatched with palms.
The landscape outside of huts might be desert or tropical
island. Everything I wanted my reader to know about the
constructions I was referring to was contained in the word
'whare' – the materials, the manner of construction, shape,
the landscape outside. I did describe the materials, but so
much of what I wanted to say was embodied in that word
– a word that stands only for something that belongs irrevo-
cably here.

And that is what te reo gives us, not only through meaning,
but sound. I love to read fiction by Indian and Chinese writers,
which is often scattered with words I don't know. Invariably,
context gives meaning, though I know that what I imagine
might not be the fullest sense of the word. But what these
words also give me is the sounds of the culture and the place
they come from. I value these words because they carry a
cultural resonance that cannot be gained by description or
explanation in English.

Consider this poem by one of New Zealand's most extraordinary poets to his friend, one of New Zealand's most extraordinary visual artists:

**Hotere**
by Hone Tuwhare[*]

When you offer only three
vertical lines precisely drawn
and set into a dark pool of lacquer
it is a visual kind of starvation:

and even though my eyeballs
roll up and over to peer inside
myself, when I reach the beginning
of your eternity I say instead: hell
let's have another feed of mussels

*Like, I have to think about it, man*

When you stack horizontal lines
into vertical columns which appear
to advance, recede, shimmer and wave
like exploding packs of cards
I merely grunt and say: well, if it
is not a famine, it's a feast

*I have to roll another smoke, man*

---

[*] From *Small Holes in the Silence: Collected Works*, Godwit, Random House, 2011, p. 100. Many thanks to the estate of Hone Tuwhare for permission to reproduce this poem.

But when you score a superb orange
circle on a purple thought-base
I shake my head and say: hell, what
is this thing called *aroha*

*Like I'm euchred man, I'm eclipsed.*

In the second to last line, Tuwhare plays on the 1929 song by jazz musician Cole Porter, 'What Is This Thing Called Love?' It's a magnificent poem, Tuwhare's trademark colloquial wit mixed with an astute tribute to his friend's art. Throughout, a tension between more formal abstract descriptions of the art and the warm, loose moments of friendship is maintained, until that resounding question: What is this thing called *aroha*? It's a good question – what is aroha and how does it differ from love – because by changing one word of a well-known line, Tuwhare draws attention to the inability of the word 'love' to encompass the world suggested by the word 'aroha'. It's much more than that, of course, but in the context of this discussion, his choice to use one Māori word in a poem in English shows how no other word would do.

Aroha is not romantic love, of course, nor is it parental love or familial love, though it could encompass all those things. Perhaps 'empathy' is the closest English word to aroha. Compassion. Aroha says: I see you, I know your pain, I'm here, I understand your world. You understand mine. I stand beside you. I don't know what it meant for Tuwhare when he placed it in this poem, but it seems to say: there is no greater thing than this.

A lecture I recently attended addressed briefly the topic of glossaries and why a writer might choose not to use them. This is something I've already touched on and thought about a lot in relation to my own work, but the lecturer, Dougal McNeill, had a succinct and eloquent way of putting it: A glossary, he said, creates a hierarchy of the familiar and unfamiliar. It highlights an area of 'foreignness' that 'normal' people won't understand. He was referring to the work of the late Chinua Achebe, who did not translate Nigerian Igbo words in his English language novel *Things Fall Apart* in 1958.

Thus, if we make glossaries for Māori words or italicise them, we separate them as abnormal, foreign, and not part of our literary landscape. We make them secondary to English. Patricia Grace is perhaps the writer most well known for refusing to explain or highlight her use of Māori words in English language texts this way.

But what responsibility does this present for the rest of us? One reaction is for non-Māori-speaking readers to say they feel excluded when Māori words are not translated. This is almost never the intention of the writing, but perhaps it does perform the function of prompting or discomforting the reader enough to act (or complain). If a New Zealand reader cannot understand simple words or phrases in one of the official languages of his or her country, should he or she not attempt to learn? If there are things that can only be said in Māori, should the writer be compelled to act as translator as well, even knowing the translation is likely to be inadequate?

And should we want them to? What do we lose if we con-stantly want things spelled out for us, if we refuse to just listen to the sounds the words make, and absorb their meaning from the story around them?

The use and acceptance of te reo Māori in English language writing has the same purpose and effect as choosing to call yourself 'Pākehā' rather than a 'New Zealand European'. We create a new English that only belongs to this place. Chinua

Achebe wrote of the same thing in Africa in 1975. He had been given this English language, he said, and he would use it to communicate to a wider audience. But in doing so, the English would not go unchanged. It would be made to commune with his ancestral home and carry the weight of his contemporary African experience. When we incorporate words like 'whare' and 'aroha' into our writing, we do so recognising that 'hut' and 'love' would not encompass the wholeness of our experience. We make our most common language carry the weight of our ancestral and contemporary realities.

My offering here today is small. I have given you a tiny handful of words. But if anything I have said today has prompted you to think about the substantial richness of those few words, consider then what would be gained from achieving some fluency in te reo. If the word 'whenua' can show the symbolic relationship Māori have with land, consider the insights that might be gained from a thorough knowledge of all aspects of Māori communication. Imagine how your point of view, or our collective relationships with each other, might be transformed by a deeper understanding of the indigenous language of Aotearoa. Imagine then, if someone asks 'what is this thing called aroha?' Perhaps the answer would be, in whatever language: 'I get you mate, I understand.'

# Rachel Buchanan
# There's a Buried Forest on My Land

In May 2012, my father, my youngest daughter and I turned off Eltham Road and into a farm gate. We were looking for our ancestral Taranaki iwi land. Our whānau has owned this land for many generations but none of we Buchanans had ever walked on it. Just inside the gate, there was a modest house and a big shed. A tractor and a ute were parked out the front of the shed. A thick-set, bald man in a checked shirt was leaning against the ute. He was smiling and relaxed. A silky brindle dog did circles at his feet.

I felt nervous. Dad was nervous too. Dad parked the car, hopped out and shook the farmer's hand. The dairy farmer's name is Karl Mullin. Dad went to school with Karl's dad John. Both of them were boarders at St Joe's in Masterton. Much later, in early middle-age, the two men had met again when my father, a paediatrician at Taranaki Base Hospital, had treated one of John's sons, a boy of two or three with a life-threatening condition. The baby had subsequently died. 'I remember you,' Karl said to my father. 'You cared for my brother.' No doubt John Mullin had remembered all this too, when Dad had phoned him the week before to ask for permission to visit Orimupiko No. 22. Dad had not mentioned the sick child to me at all. Medical ethics would prevent it.

First published in full as 'Orimupiko 22 and the Haze of History', *Journal of New Zealand Studies* 16, 2013, pp. 66–78.

But the dead child was there with us now, just for a moment. Karl's face softened. I saw a shadow of something, sadness or fear. I don't know what. My father said nothing. My daughter, Frances, just six, put her plump wee hand in mine and looked at her feet. Her white-gold hair was tied back but pieces had escaped and the Taranaki damp had frizzed these strands into a fuzzy halo around her dear pink face.

Karl offered to show us around. 'That's your land,' he said. 'It runs from the fenceline down to the river.'

Our eyes followed Karl's finger, taking in the paddocks, the fences, the ditches, the small stand of remnant native bush and the lovely curl of the river – the Waiaua – wrapped around the southern edge of our small patch of Ōpunake. This bit of land was excellent, Karl said. The best in the district. It was flat and fertile and free from lahars.

On a clear day, the mountain would loom up over the farm but today he was covered in clouds, from foothills to summit. 'The mountain doesn't come out for visitors,' Karl said pleasantly. It was time to get moving. Frances and I sat in the back of the ute and Dad and Karl hopped in the front. Karl's dog Oscar panted up the back. The dog leapt up to try to lick Frances' soft little neck. Frances giggled happily. I looked out the window as if in a dream. Karl knew everything and I knew nothing. Karl knew the boundaries of our block and the boundaries of the other Māori blocks too. The rest of the farm had been West Coast Settlement Reserve land too, he said looking over his shoulder back towards the mountain, but his father, John, had 'converted' it some time ago so the Mullins owned it outright.

I did not have the words to explain what I felt. Perhaps I was happy. Or maybe I was meek and grateful. Certainly there were other sensations too: anger, sorrow, rage; total disbelief.

There is certainly no term in the English language to express my situation. I was less than nothing. I was an invited guest on my own land. The tenant was the host. The land that was 'ours' was, manifestly, 'his'. The land was an orphan, adopted by his family, abandoned by ours.

We bumped along down towards the river then back up the hill again. On the top of an incline, just above the bush and the rusted rim of a car, a tattooed man chopped up large, black rātā logs. Karl used the logs for firewood. They burnt really well. 'If you dig down deep enough here, you'll find natives,' Karl explained.

Similar trees lay beneath the entire block, making it difficult to dig ditches or lay drains. 'Something came through here,' he said. 'A big landslide and it pushed all of them over.' The trees all pointed in the same direction, seawards. There's a buried forest beneath our land. Later, when I mentioned the day to Frances, she was enthusiastic about the time she spent 'on farmer Karl's farm'. Oscar the dog made a big impression but so did the hawk we saw as we left.

### Where are they now?

The accountants in Whanganui had sent the slip of paper to Dad and seventy-one others. The slip said: 'Attached is a list of owners in Orimupiko 22 Trust that we do not have addresses for. If you know where any of these people live could you please send us their details in the enclosed envelope. Thank You.'

When I looked at the twenty-one names on this list, I saw birds pattering about on a wet, windy beach. The birds were all very far apart. The weather was so bad that they could not see further than their feet. The rain had played a trick on them.

First the birds could not see the flock and then they forgot that the flock was even there.

## Spicks and specks

Go to the Ministry of Justice. Then go to the Māori Land Court. Then go to Māori Land Online. Type in Orimupiko No. 22. A map will pop up. The block is shaded dark grey. To the north, the map is white, just as Karl said. Look left, more grey. Look down, grey again. Roll the mouse back and still more grey appears in varying forms: fat rectangles, skinny oblongs, boxes with deckle edges, a triangle, a block shaped like a beak, tiny dots and squiggles right by the sea. All pieces for a puzzle that we can no longer complete because there are too many bits missing, whited out, emptied out, alienated, confiscated, sold.

## 1975

My cousin Paul Walker met my grandmother Rawinia once. It was 1975 and Paul, his mum Doreen, and Flossie were three of the owners of Orimupiko 22 who had been summoned to Wellington for a meeting about the block. Everyone had to come, apparently. If people failed to show up, then the land would be sold or taken. 'I remember the day quite well,' Paul told me, 'because it was the day the land march arrived in Wellington.'

## Play-time

The 1915 Partition Order for Orimupiko 22 was issued under Section 21 of the West Coast Settlement Reserves Amendment

Act 1913 and 1914 and the Native Land Act 1909. I have counted up all the relevant legislation for Block 22. My list begins with the New Zealand Settlements Act of 1863 and ends with the Māori Reserved Lands Amendment Act 1997. The list is very long but almost certainly incomplete. My land is a play in twenty-one Acts. Stop playing with my land.

### Trustee

Robert Hamerton was the first public trustee for the West Coast Settlement Reserves. He had arrived in New Plymouth, from Lancashire, in 1854, aged sixteen. Six years later, he became an ensign for the Taranaki Rifle Volunteers, rising, eventually, to the rank of captain. The New Zealand Settlements Act of 1863 confiscated most land in Taranaki. Māori were never given any of the promised reserves, a failing that the non-violent activist community at Parihaka attempted to highlight and address. In 1880 the recommendations of the West Coast Commission led to an Act that awarded 201,395 acres to 5289 individuals. The former soldier, Hamerton, was put in charge of the reserve land. He held a pen instead of a rifle but the result was quite similar. Some land was leased in perpetuity and other parcels of land – such as Orimupiko 22 – were subject to shorter term arrangements. These leases are little land mines embedded in Taranaki Māori families, including my own. But they are also a rope that links us, intimately, with Parihaka and its revolutionary leaders whose simple message was: Land, Mine!

### The writer's block

I have made my living from writing since I was eighteen.

I often find writing a challenge but two careers – journalism and academia – mean that writer's block is not a luxury I have been able to afford for too long. Until 2012, the year I discovered my very own Writer's Block, Orimupiko 22, and a block order file to go with it.

Block order files are kept at Māori Land Court offices. The court is unique; it is the only one in the world structured around whakapapa. There are booklets to explain how it all works: trust, succession, leases and all the rest. The opening paragraph of each booklet is the same. The second sentence says: 'The special bond between Māori people and the land is recognised by the Māori Land Court, and the records held by this Court form an invaluable part of the whakapapa of all Māori.' A special bond is a phrase that describes the relationship that a grandparent enjoys with a favoured mokopuna but is certainly not a phrase that describes the feelings I had when I visited my land in Ōpunake.

In its discussion of the impact of raupatu and 'land reform' in Taranaki (*The Taranaki Report: Kaupapa Tuatahi*, 1996) the Waitangi Tribunal observed that: 'Ancestral laws on how lands were held, allocated and inherited were displaced by Government laws that brought Māori into the Government system.'

While my Pākehā ancestors were building up a farming dynasty in Southland, my Māori ones in Taranaki were prevented from making any decisions at all about their land in Ōpunake, land they had occupied for hundreds of years. My mother, Mary English, grew up at Rosedale, the English family homestead in down-country Southland. Mum told me that the farm was set up five generations ago 'when my great-grandfather bought the land from Mr Rose'. It has been handed down from father to sons ever since. With every generation, my mother's family built their wealth and their attachment. With every generation in my Māori family, wealth and attachment diminished. As the Tribunal put it, in the Taranaki report:

'A more particular prejudice was caused by the increased alienation of Māori land, multiple land ownership, fragmentation of title, title dispersal, absentee ownership, uneconomic interests, missing owners, unbankable titles, tenant farming, rent dispersal and administrative control by Māori Land Court, the Māori Trustee, and, later, the Māori Affairs Department. In social and cultural terms, Māori land has been made an illusory and meaningless asset.'

This statement induces a kind of writer's block in me. What do I do with it? Is it true that Orimupiko 22 is an illusory, meaningless and under-performing asset? Am I prepared to let this statement be true?

To escape the injustice of the recent history of Orimupiko 22 and the 27,000-plus other blocks of remaining Māori freehold land, I can take a longer view of historical time. For example, I can step back 7000 years to the moment when the southwest section of Te Maunga Taranaki's summit collapsed. Volcanic ash and debris poured down the side of the mountain. Forests were felled, hills destroyed, rivers filled and still the lahar kept flowing, out on past the present coastline at Ōpunake. This eruption felled the forest on Orimupiko 22. Volcanologists describe it as a 'new' event. The time of history is a shimmering slick on the surface of the time of the volcano. A comforting thought.

### Farming
Like so many other blocks of Māori freehold land, Orimupiko 22 is just a speck but put it together with the 27,307 other

specks and you have 1.466 million hectares or 5.66 per cent of New Zealand's land mass. This land is now under intense political and economic scrutiny. In 2012 the National Government announced a review of Te Ture Whenua Māori Act 1993 and flagged its intention to 'improve the performance and productivity of Māori land'. The government says 80 per cent of Māori freehold land is 'underdeveloped or ignored by some disengaged owners'.

My research into Orimupiko 22 illuminates some of the reasons for this owner 'disengagement' and it has posed profound professional and personal challenges for me as a historian and as a Taranaki uri. The chaos created by the Taranaki wars and their aftermath has knifed time, split it apart, hazed everything up and the more research I did, the foggier things got.

The war stories that link real tangata to actual bits of whenua can be excruciating, sad and tortuous, but the stories can also reveal persistence and vision. I remain hopeful that the fog will clear. In the meantime, I have become a farmer, too, digging through records, letting some air into them, waiting to see what might pop up. This is one way, at least, that I am able to care for my land.

# Simon Wilson
## Mutton

My grandfather was a farmer. He fell off his horse once, gashing open his thigh. He rode home and sewed it up himself. He set very high standards.

When I knew them, Clem Wilson and his wife Ida, they dressed like English aristocracy: Clem had a clipped moustache, wore a lot of tweed, brogues, never went out without a bow tie. My grandmother, Ida, basically looked at all times like the Queen Mother.

Clem drove an impeccably maintained Morris Oxford – or Austin Cambridge. I am ashamed to say I cannot remember which. They were, after all, identical but for the badge on the front. The condition of that car was the key to my grandfather. He did everything perfectly. The garage sorted just so. His bed, tightly tucked at all times, unlike my grandmother's, next to it, which was a warm and blowzy mess.

He was in Egypt during the war, and after that, in 1919, he married Ida and they got themselves a little farm, high in the valleys of inland Hawke's Bay. For her it was a rebound: she'd been sweet on a boy named Willoughby Willcox, who was killed, I think at Passchendaele. She always said she came over all funny one day in the kitchen, and discovered later that was the moment he had died.

First told live at SURVIVAL: True Stories Told Live for Christchurch, Auckland Museum, 30 October 2010; broadcast on Radio New Zealand National, 26 December 2012; and published online by the New Zealand Book Council (www.bookcouncil.org.nz/truestories).

When I was born, the eldest son of her eldest son, on her birthday, she pleaded with my mother to give me his name. I would have been Willoughby Willcox Wilson. My mother was a splendidly independent woman, sometimes.

It was bitter in the valley. The air so damp Ida could never get the clothes dry. The land so steep, Clem couldn't get stock onto it. Snow in winter, floods in spring. The cold, the heavy bush and the desolate scrub. Quardle oodle ardle wardle doodle, oh yes.

Clem learned to do everything. Horses, stock, finances, buildings and repairs. Be a married man.

Ida wasn't used to it – her family had lived in South Africa, where it was easier. When I knew her, she always left food on her plate. Why? we used to ask. She would say it was for the black children in the kitchen.

In that Hawke's Bay valley, she learned how to carve a sheep and serve it three times a day. How to be a farm labourer. How to deal with miscarriage. There is – there was – a bigger family secret about those days, perhaps more than one, but they never told a soul, and it died with them. A stillborn birth? Some awful violence? Maybe just the cumulative wretchedness. They gutted it out for as long as they could, but it beat them, and after a few years they crawled out of the valley and down to the coast, where Clem became a hired hand and my father was born.

\*

Dad was two when Clem got a job managing another farm, way down on the coast of the southern Wairarapa. There was no road in, and they arrived during summer, my granddad on horseback, mother and child in a wagon, bumping their way down the baked-dry river bed.

Tora is beautiful, when you're in the right frame of mind, but it's also bleak and brutal. There's a flat coastal plain before the land changes its mind and soars straight into the sky. The trees stretch out along the ground, everything is full of salt and gritty sand, and the wind blows all the time. The farm was enormous, running away inland, collapsing into gullies, folding itself over ridge after ridge. Riding the perimeter could take you away for days. The sea rolls past, too wild for swimming. The bays are full of stingrays. In summer, the sun burns fiercely. In winter, the storms rage for days on end.

They had a big farm crew, holed up in that little corner of the universe. A boat came a few times a year, to take out the wool and bring in supplies. There was no jetty. They swung the enormous bales into the rowboats with winches, pulleys and hooks. My grandfather was a tyrant. It was his job to make sure no arms were broken, no legs crushed. He had a perfect record, more or less.

They ate mutton, three times a day, and what vegetables my grandmother and the farm cook could grow. The Māori shearing gangs, when they came through, feasted on the crayfish and kina and pāua. My family, and the Pākehā farmhands, stuck to the mutton.

The homestead was large without being grand. Walking around it now, it feels like it was underwater for years: wallpaper peels from the walls, the floors undulate, it's desperately shabby. It was the manager's house, and you can see that effort was once made, but it wasn't a family seat. No one was laying in a tradition for the generations to come.

Twice a year the owner came calling. The Riddifords lived way down the coast at Orongorongo, in a homestead so beautiful it even had a ballroom. The Riddifords owned half the southern Wairarapa, and quite a bit of the Hutt Valley and

Manawatū, and the old man, Eric Riddiford, would arrive on horseback, bathe and relax in the rooms kept by my grandmother for his exclusive use, put on the fresh clean clothes she kept for him, dine with my grandparents on their best mutton, with crockery and silverware and linen kept exclusively for him, and then shut himself up for a long night with my grandfather in his little study, where they pored over the accounts.

Riddiford chain-smoked cigars in that little room. Clem did not smoke, and he never said a word about it.

*

The Depression cost my grandfather the chance to own another farm. But he had a job. He was one of the lucky ones.

And he had a family. It was a dark and stormy night when my uncle Godfrey was born. Seriously, it was so dark and stormy a coastal steamer ran aground on the point. My grandmother moaned and screamed her way through the labour, while out in the howling black night men fought for their lives among the surf-pounded rocks. It's a good story, one of my family's classics. I checked the dates a few years ago. It's quite close: the shipwreck and the birth were in the same week.

The wreck was a boon for my grandparents. The wood from the boat was turned into furniture. All the silverware we ate the Sunday mutton with when we visited was foraged from the wreck, including the bone-handled knives. I have a pepper grinder, still one of the finest tools in my kitchen, that came straight from the captain's table eighty-something years ago.

The kids grew up and the war came, and my father flew planes off aircraft carriers and afterwards volunteered to bomb the New Territories in Hong Kong with DDT, to wipe out the malaria. I think it was his version of sewing up his own leg. But neither he nor my uncle were what my grandparents had expected. They liked farm life well enough, but they were drawn by the siren call of the age: the world was waiting to be built anew.

Quite young, my dad had decided to be an architect, so at school he was called Archie, and after the war he trained in Auckland under Vernon Brown. And my uncle Godfrey, having at first set his sights on being a journalist, had an epiphany one day and went off to become a vicar. We called him Uncle God, though not to his face.

*

There was a third child. My aunt Joan, also born at Tora, in circumstances no one ever talked about. Known as Jo.

When she was little, the family visited the lighthouse at Castlepoint, and while Jo was up on the reef of sharp, fossil-filled rocks, a giant wave knocked her over. She slid, scraping the skin from her body, all the way down into the lagoon.

When I knew her, her face and body were covered in warts. That was the family story – the one we were told as kids – of how she got the warts.

Jo was 'slow', quite possibly on account of something that happened during her birth. Slow and therefore under-edu-cated. My grandparents kept her close, they insisted on it, and when they retired to Masterton she lived with them until they died. She had her father's disposition: perfectionism in him became fixation in her.

She loved Elvis Presley. In her room, which was white and frilly, the walls and even the ceiling were covered in photos of Elvis. She played his records all the time. She went to his movies, every day when they were on, which was quite often. He made – I've looked this up – thirty-one. When Elvis married Priscilla, Jo wailed and rent her clothes and was inconsolable for months. I saw her once with a picture of Priscilla. She grabbed her scissors and stabbed at it.

She had friends in town, at the radio station, in the shops. Among the police. The Wart Lady was famous in Masterton, in more than one way. She took to stalking the streets, accosting men. Inappropriate behaviour was not the sort of thing anyone knew how to talk about. There would be phone calls.

My grandfather would fasten the bow tie, pull on his tweed jacket with the leather patches, head for town to collect her in the Morris Oxford, or Austin Cambridge. There were tears, and fury. Clem was a quiet, still man, but Jo had a raging temper. So he learned life is not something only to be lived in the dry pockets of order. He learned about the snotty-nosed life, the shuddering, arms-wrapped-tightly-round despair of an unfair life.

*Elvis is dead.*

*The men in the pub are horrible.*

*You won't let me do anything.*

And then they smoothed things over, hushed things up. They learned to manage, the three of them.

My father set up in town as an architect and started his own family. I was born there. But we soon ran off to Wellington. The grandparents visited the awful city once, and drove the wrong way up a motorway off-ramp. In the Morris Oxford. Worse: Uncle God forsook his old-world high-church roots and became a liberal vicar. He fronted for the Defence and Aid Fund for Southern Africa, despite my grandmother's fond memories of leaving food on the plate for the little black boys. And yet she coped.

In 1965, when I was ten and loved my rugby, Jo took me to see the Springboks play Wairarapa Bush, captained by Brian Lochore. I remember the sharp shadows of the players in the bright winter sunshine, the blond locks of Dawie de Villiers and Lochore's systematic, unbelievably blatant cheating. Jo disappeared behind the stands for much of the match.

Five years later I was fifteen, with long hair and flared pants, and it was the time of the All Blacks tour of South Africa, when Sid Going and Bryan Williams were designated 'honorary whites'. I argued with my grandmother about it and she hated that, but she continued to manage.

*

Clem and Ida Wilson. They wanted a farm. And kids to inherit it. And a world that made sense to them.

Clem believed in doing everything just so, but did it make a difference? His sons rushed to join the great national task of making cities work, and his grandkids insisted, when we stayed with them, on making him watch Peter Sinclair on the TV. And he and Ida got a daughter who did everything not perfectly, but catastrophically, and who taught them the power of love more fiercely than either of their finickity high-achieving sons. And they rose, wonderfully, to that.

And they got a modernist house to retire into, designed by my father. It was his tribute to them, a precisely designed masterpiece of open-plan living mixed with private bedrooms. His way of saying, I love that you have come from an old world and enabled me to live well in the new one, and I want to make this new world a place for you to live well in too.

It was set in large grounds with fruit trees and a stream and long borders of hydrangeas, and even a little paddock with one sheep. And though it was the antithesis of all the closed rooms of the Tora homestead, they managed, and then they learned to love it.

There was a little wood-fired range in the kitchen, for old time's sake, although when my grandmother roasted the Sunday mutton she always used the proper stove.

You survive until you don't. In his eighties, Clem got sick and died, and within six months Ida lay down and died too. It wasn't the mutton.

The way I remember them is in their tweeds, tootling into town in their Morris Oxford, or Austin Cambridge, raking the gravel, bending stiffly to pick plums from the lawn with 'Blue Suede Shoes' pounding from Jo's open window. Living in grace.

# Keith Ng
## The Sound of Thunder

My grandfather, in his teens, almost starved to death. His father did starve to death. Before my great-grandfather died, he told my grandfather to leave his two young sisters behind. My grandfather buried him alone, and three days later, the elder of his two sisters died. He left his youngest sister with a relative, and she too starved soon after.

My first memory of my grandparents' place is of a nice apartment on a leafy street in Hong Kong. That was the world I was born into, the only world I knew. I understood that people starved in Africa, but that was somebody else's world.

My grandfather died when I was four. I wasn't told the details of why he came to Hong Kong until I was well into my twenties. It's a strange thing to discover that the world as I knew it had barely existed for a decade when I was born; that my family – middle-class professionals who would rarely leave a plate unfinished – was a product of hardships that don't seem possible in our world.

But having understood how much the world can change in two generations, I don't understand how people can believe that their world will never change. I don't understand how people can look at the world the Intergovernmental Panel on Climate Change describes, mouth the words 'climate change is a very serious issue', and simply assume that the same world

First published on Keith's blog OnPoint, on Public Address, April 2014 (http://publicaddress.net/onpoint/sound-of-thunder/).

of flat whites and iPhones will be inherited by their children. I don't understand how people can accept scientists describing a world with food and water insecurity, with freak heat waves and droughts and hurricanes, and never consider what that world would entail beyond vague abstractions.

Your children may not enjoy a world of growth and prosperity. Your grandchildren may not live in a world of safety and security. Your great-grandchildren may not have three meals a day.

Sometimes I wonder what my great-grandfather's dying thought was. He was, at one point, an engineer of sorts. He built fish traps for the village, or maybe they were shrimp traps; from what I gather, it was a system of dams that caught stuff when the tide went in and out. He was a clever guy.

He understood the catastrophe that was coming when the Japanese invaded, and then when China descended into civil war. He tried to prepare. He stashed food away for a rainy day, but he got sick and by the time that rainy day came, the food he had stashed had spoiled or been stolen.

Maybe there was more he could have done. Maybe there wasn't. But I doubt either thought would have given him any comfort as he considered how utterly and catastrophically he had failed his children.

## David Winter
# The Origin and Extinction of Species

When people ask me to explain my PhD research, the shortest answer I can provide is 'I use genetic tools to study evolution'. Occasionally I've caught myself expanding on that by saying 'I'm interested in the questions, not the particular animals I study.' Paraphrased, that becomes something like, 'Oh sure, I study Pacific land snails, but for all I care they're just little bags of genes that help me answer questions.'

But that's a lie. You can't work on animals without having them affect you. When I started my PhD, I had no particular love of snails, but now I'm a complete snail fan-boy and I frequently find myself preaching on the wonders of life as a terrestrial mollusc to people whose only mistake was to ask me what I do for a living. Did you know most slugs retain the remnants of their shells? Or that almost all snail shells coil to the right? Or that mating in many land snail species only proceeds after one snail has stabbed the other with a 'love dart'? And then there's the sad tale of the Society Islands partulids.

Believe it or not, land snails are one of the character-istic animals of Pacific Islands. Anak Krakatau, which appeared in 1927, is so young it's still smouldering, and yet it

First published on David's blog The Atavism, December 2010 (http://theatavism. blogspot.co.nz/2010/12/sunday-spinelessness-origin-and.html); and reprinted in *The Best Science Writing Online, 2012*, ed. Jennifer Ouellette (New York: Scientific American/Farrar, Straus and Giroux, 2012), pp. 276–80.

already has its own native land snail species. Rapa Nui (Easter Island), which is arguably the most isolated island in the Pacific, had its own land snail fauna back when it had forests. It's not entirely clear how these unlikely colonists find their way to islands. Darwin was so interested in the question that he, ever the experimentalist, stuck snails to ducks' feet to see if they'd survive an inter-island journey. Birds have indeed been shown to carry snails great distances, but windblown leaves are probably a more common mode of conveyance.

We might not know exactly how snails get to islands, but we know what happens once they establish themselves. The land snails of the Pacific include some of the most outrageous explosions of diversity in the biological world. Chief among these evolutionary radiations were the partulid snails of the Society Islands (the French Polynesian archipelago that includes Tahiti). Partulids are very elegant tree snails that form part of the land snail fauna across most of Polynesia; in the Societies, they made up most of the land snail fauna. In total, the tiny islands had fifty-eight species of these snails, with each of the main islands having its own endemic forms.

The Society Islands land snails were a marvel all by themselves, but they have also been an extraordinary resource for scientists. The first person to seriously take up their study was the American embryologist and evolutionary biologist Henry Crampton. Crampton was working at the turn of the twentieth century, a time at which the mechanisms underlying genetics and evolution were very much up for debate, and he hoped Tahitian and Moorean partulids could help set the story straight. Crampton's monographs are famous (at least among people who spend their lives thinking about snails) for their detail.* He collected and measured over 200,000 shells, then calculated summary statistics for each species, each site and each measurement. By hand. To eight decimal places.

The massive tables he drew up (there are more than a hundred pages of them in the Moorean monograph) might seem like an old-fashioned, descriptive way to do biology. But in many ways Crampton was ahead of his time. For one, he was a Darwinist when not every evolutionist was. By the end of the nineteenth century, Darwin had convinced the world of the *fact* of evolution, but relatively few naturalists bought his *theory* of how evolutionary change happened.

The anti-Darwinian theories that prospered during the so-called 'eclipse of Darwinism' placed very little importance on the variation within species. The orthogenesists and the Lamarckians thought evolution had a driving force, pushing species towards perfection. In their scheme, variation within a species was deviance from the mainstream of evolution and was quickly stamped out by natural selection. The Lamarckians didn't deny natural selection; they just said it couldn't be a creative force. Similarly, saltationists thought that large-scale evolutionary changes occurred in a single generation, and that the small changes you see in populations were of no consequence in the grand scheme of evolution.

Crampton realised that, in a Darwinian world, variation within populations was the raw material of evolution. He was obsessive about measuring his shells because he knew he could use the data to understand where species came from.

---

*　Henry E. Crampton, 'Studies on the variation, distribution and evolution of the genus *Partula*. The species inhabiting Tahiti', *Carnegie Institution of Washington* 228 (1916): 1–311; 'Studies on the Variation, Distribution, and Evolution of the Genus *Partula*. The Species Inhabiting Moorea', *Carnegie Institution of Washington Publications* 410 (1932): 1–335.

In particular, he was able to show that isolated populations of the same species varied from each other. This finding makes sense in light of Darwin's theory, since species arise from populations evolving away from each other; but is harder to fit into progressive theories of evolution, in which you'd expect different populations of the same species to follow the same trajectory.

Crampton's results influenced people like Dobzhansky, Mayr and Huxley who helped to reestablish Darwinism as the principal theory of evolution in the modern evolutionary synthesis. But Crampton also predicted what was arguably the most important development in evolutionary theory since the modern synthesis. In the middle of the twentieth century, evolutionary genetics was defined by a single debate. The 'classical' school held that populations in the wild would have almost no genetic variation, because for every gene there would be one 'best' version and every member of the population would have two copies of that gene. Against the classical school, the 'balance' school argued that, quite often, there would be no single best gene, and organisms would do better having two different versions of the same gene. The balancers thought natural selection would keep lots of different versions of maybe 10 per cent of a species' genes.

Both schools assumed natural selection was such a pervasive force that it would dictate the way populations were made up; they just disagreed on what would result from it. They were both spectacularly wrong. When scientists started being able to measure the genetic diversity of populations in the 1960s, it became clear that almost every single gene had multiple different versions. Now, in the post-genomic age, there is a database with 30 million examples of one sort of genetic variant among humans.

Faced with the overwhelming variation he recorded in partulid shells, Crampton had argued that natural selection didn't have a damn thing to do with it. Snails isolated from each other by a mountain weren't adapting to their local habitat, they just varied with respect to traits that had no influence on their survival. The fact that two populations were isolated meant each would follow its own path, and thus two populations could drift apart from each other. Faced with the overwhelming genetic variation coming from studies in the 1960s, Motoo Kimura proposed the neutral theory of molecular evolution. Kimura's explanation was the same as Crampton's: that almost all of the variation we see at genetic level has no bearing on the success or failure of organisms, so the frequency of different variants drifts around at random. The neutral theory is at the heart of a lot of modern evolutionary genetics – and Crampton had understood the underlying principle fifty years before we knew we needed it.

Crampton worked on the partulids for the best part of thirty years. At the end of his last monograph, on the Moorean species, Crampton said he'd got as far as his measurements could take him, and it was time for someone to study their genetics. This took a bit longer than Crampton might have hoped, but in the 1960s two leading geneticists took up the study of his snails. James Murray from Virginia and Bryan Clarke from Nottingham spent almost twenty years working in what they called, in more than one paper, the perfect 'museum and laboratory' in which to study the origin of species. Their work helped scientists understand, among other things, how ecology can contribute to the formation of new species, and what happens to species when they hybridise with others from time to time.

Then, in 1984, Murray and Clarke had to write the most heartbreaking scientific paper I've ever read. It's written in the careful prose scientists use to talk to each other, but the message it delivered was devastating:

> In an attempt to control the numbers of the giant African snail, *Achatina fulica*, which is an agricultural pest, a carnivorous snail, *Euglandina rosea*, has been introduced into Moorea. It is spreading across the island at the rate of about 1.2 km per year, eliminating the endemic *Partula*. One species is already extinct in the wild. Extrapolating the rate of spread of *Euglandina*, it is expected that all the remaining taxa (possibly excepting *P. exigua*) will be eliminated by 1986–1987.[*]

*Euglandina rosea* is better known as the rosy wolf snail, or 'cannibal snail'. It senses the mucous trails of other snails, tracks them down and eats them. It's not clear if the wolf snail had any effect on the pest species it was introduced to control, but it had a huge impact on the indigenous partulids. By the time Murray and Clarke wrote their paper, *E. rosea* had already done for one species and was too well established to control. All the scientists could do was watch as human stupidity and molluscan hunger slowly (at the rate of 1.2 kilometres per year) destroyed the species they'd been studying for twenty years, and to which Crampton had dedicated fifty years of his life.

[*] Bryan Clarke, James Murray, and Michael S. Johnson, 'The Extinction of Endemic Species by a Program of Biological Control', *Pacific Science* 38, no. 2 (1984): 97–104.

The same slow torture played itself out in Tahiti and then the rest of the Society Islands: of the fifty-eight named species there are now five alive in the wild.

Crampton's hundreds of pages of painstakingly assembled tables should have been the starting point from which the evolution of the partulids could have been tracked. Murray and Clarke's natural laboratory should still be open and should be taking advantage of a new generation of technologies that might be able to reveal the genetic and genomic changes that occur when a new species arises. Extinction is a natural part of life, and the fate of all species eventually – but when it's driven by human short-sightedness and robs us of not just a wonderful product of nature but a window through which we might have understood nature's workings, it's very hard to write about.

There is a tiny scrap of good news in this story. The partulids are no longer an iconic genus in the study of evolution, but they have become the pandas of invertebrate conservation. Murray and Clarke were able to get fifteen of the partulid species off the islands and into zoos and labs across the northern hemisphere. Breeding programmes have been successful, and new lab-based studies come out from time to time. The relict populations back in the Societies don't have nearly the range they used to, but it appears they've held on to most of their original genetic variation. Perhaps, one day, *Euglandina* can be taken care of and some of the partulids can have their islands back.

# Claire Browning
## Spring Forward

I.

I live in a town with a railway, a river, and two roads running through it. To the west stand the Rimutaka hills, the Forest Park, and the Pigeon Bush Reserve. To the south lies Lake Wairarapa, with its birds and wetlands. On the north side of town is the Domain, where bush huddles on the side of the hill, and one lonely pine looks out to the horizon.

There are trees on scraps of public land around the town. The Dorset Square park. A battered rest area by the reserve, where kererū congregate in flocks when the tree lucerne is flowering.

I don't know how long I'll live in this town. People come and go here. The old ones die and the young ones leave. The wind, when it blows, howls down like a runaway train.

But the wind doesn't always blow; and there seems no reason why Featherston shouldn't be a pocket between some very special wildlife places filled with trees and birds – except, there's no money here to do it. In Featherston, like the wind and the roads, people just drive through on their way somewhere else.

But I would like to offer it some trees, because I love trees, and I believe that trees change things; that this town could

Written over six years from 2009 to 2014, and first published in part on Pundit (pundit.co.nz/blogs/claire-browning). Now collected on Claire's blog Wild Life (http://wild-life.kiwi.nz/).

do with some fingers of green reaching out into it, and who knows what might happen after that. I'd like to see veins of trees spreading out around the town, offering shade and shelter, some food for birds, and food for people too – and I think, in a few years, this might become a beautiful thing, or at least, a better thing.

Even if it does nothing for the town, if people neither notice nor care, it would still be a gift for the wildlife: for the kererū who come to my plum and wild cherry trees, and rest in the sycamore tree on contemplative summer afternoons. If they – and the silvereyes, bellbirds and tūī who live around here too – had miro, karaka and wineberry to feast upon and rest in, what happy birds they'd be.

## II.

The first memory of my garden is touched by autumn sunshine. Fast forward – through dilapidation, a weedy wilderness, interminable expense – to the last weekend in July. July slipped into August, and the plum trees slipped into blossom. My garden story begins in August; July is its blank first page.

I wanted, every year, to watch the garden wake up. Every year, the story rewrites itself. I wanted to grow food, and plant trees. A thicket of them filled my head.

I became a weekly pilgrim to Judy Blank's garden centre. Judy Blank specialised in heirloom fruit trees. When the pink flowering plum and white almond show their frilly knickers outside my bedroom window, I remember how it was, stumbling upon such prettiness.

Each spring I indulge in a little ritual, planting chives, dill seed, and curly parsley. The herb garden was the first garden that I planted, the day the land transferred. It was a gesture of ownership, and intent.

I watch every day for asparagus. Once, a bellbird chimed from amidst plum blossom, while I collected coffee- and cream-coloured eggs from the hens.

The plum trees have battered limbs, and wind-twisted corkscrew trunks. They are halves of a heart-shaped whole, and the soul of this garden in springtime.

The silvereyes work themselves into a twitter of delight, burying their faces in plum flowers. A kererū comes every day, to munch on unfurling leaves. After a hard night's rain, he risks the topmost east-most branch. It is a twiggy branch, and he is a dignified bird. He puffs his cream waistcoat towards the rising sun, cartoonishly, like a fat man. Sometimes he brings a friend. They will relocate in summer, a few wing beats north, to the wild cherry tree.

Last week, on holiday, I snatched moments from the weather. Torrential rain followed gales; a balmy morning segued into hail that lay on the ground in drifts. Seduced into planting lettuce seedlings, I was out that night under a freezing moon, rigging a greenhouse from old windows.

My house is on a flight path. On tranquil spring nights and summer dawns, Canada geese honk overhead. They were on the move that night, and are again this minute, as I write this in bed in the dark.

I thought for a long time about how to describe the rhythm of this garden. In the end it was simple, like breathing.

## III.

Sometimes I find it in books, sometimes in the garden; always, I find it by chance.

Monet, painter, was a gardener too. He rented a country farmhouse, with a walled vegetable garden. He espaliered apple trees to make pretty fences. He filled it with flowers, and painted them: Peony, Poppy, Iris, Lily, Rose. He thought about the light, and put blue and violet flowers in shade.

*All my money goes into my garden,* he apparently said. And, *I am in raptures.*

I have no iconic bridge to drape in mauve and white wisteria, but I have a house. Wisteria rambles up it.

Monty Don took two acres, two decades, and many thousands of words: he scaffolded a bare field into outdoor rooms, with towering hornbeam hedges, pleached limes, and box-edged gardens. He grows food with a muscular verve. He harvests sweet basil, pumpkins, and tomatoes in a *wheelbarrow*.

I have been here four years, and the planting should be finished, in my urban forest. But I am digging up and shifting things, sacrificing others. I am newly obsessed with shelter. I made a path. There was a path, once, but everything was wrong about it. This one is an epiphany.

I don't know what I will do some future winter, when there is no more room to plant trees.

So I turn again to Monty, who lives in Herefordshire, and joins me, in January, shifting things. *God!* he agonises. *I have wasted so much time moving plants from A to B in this garden. But you have to gnaw away at it until it is right.*

Monty gets up to relieve himself, and looks at his garden in the moonlight. He takes many photos of tree skeletons and bony hedges sleeping under a blanket of frost. He walks the

garden daily and nightly, and knows its geography as intimately as, I guess, his wife's.

He gives voice and shape to a secular kind of faith: of
knowing that It will happen, but not when. *This business of
making places obsesses me . . . Then one day, quite by surprise,
it is there.* Yes. Like the reassurance of finding, some way
down the garden path, as it were, that all these ideas I have
had have been good ideas, pre-loved by genius.

Last week I wandered on to some wild land on the edge of
town. The moon was a scrap of tissue; it was dusk and the
frost was coming down. I stood in a grove of tree lucerne, and
felt I was being watched – and I was, by tens, maybe hundreds,
of kererū, shimmering green and white. The sole occupants of
trees were dignified; others, doubled up, jostled and flapped.

I came back later, with my trowel, and lifted half a dozen
saplings. These are woody weeds, but I poked them into odd
corners in my own garden and prayed to recreate – some other
winter, when I cannot plant trees – even a scrap of that magic.


IV.

My mother emailed me about the Forest & Bird 'Bird of the
Year' competition. 'I voted for the Fairy Tern,' her email said.

'Was that the little lady so cleverly disguised as shells?'

'Yes,' came her reply, 'and *she didn't have many votes*.'

A short correspondence, in which my mother explains in
a handful of words why she is a conservationist. Accounting
is her job. She has a leafy shady garden through which
a weka wanders. She feeds the birds in winter. We have
never discussed this, she and I; but in her bones, and in her
heart, I think she is a conservationist.

I felt, instantly, that I was not a conservationist; I was a fraud. I myself had treated the Forest & Bird 'Bird of the Year' competition like a cheap vox pop. I voted for the morepork, because one had woken me up. I remember that I smiled, before I went back to sleep. Moonlit, my garden had looked pretty enough, my sycamore trees impressive enough, for a small owl to stop and say hello, and I gave it my vote of thanks.

I am a gardener. I like to grow food, and eat it; there's no more delicious kind. I do not like to mow the lawn. Big trees fill me with every good feeling: awe, and peace, and joy. I think I would live in a forest, if I could. I live in a town garden that is shaggy round the edges.

Once I thought: I would like to be buried under a wild apple tree, beside a running stream. The tree would blossom in springtime, fruit in autumn, feed birds in the winter. Until then, I want to make a garden that is pretty, and fruitful, and alive.

Kererū come to my plum trees in spring, fantails in the winter. Today, writing this at home, I am being kept company by a flirt of silvereyes. I am a friend of hedgehogs. Ever since I moved into this house, there has been one or other of them living beneath it. They snuffle round on summer nights, minding their business, and my own: hedgehogs eat snails, in my garden, what else they may do in the bush I do not care. The bush is far from here.

There are bees bumbling in bog sage and herbs; honey-scented butterfly bushes that bring monarchs and yellow admirals. Native praying mantises lay their frilly egg cases on the trees.

I want soil full of worms and carbon; trees breathing.

This is conservation, too.

## V.

Yesterday I knelt, and performed the last act of planting: in the space by the letterbox, a tree whose small white winter flowers smell of vanilla.

Seven years of 'sluggish plant growth and imperceptible soil improvement', waiting on Toby Hemenway's promise of the seventh year, in which:

> the garden suddenly roars into life, and seethes with greenery, fruit, blossoms and wildlife. The early establishment phase can take a few years, but then look out! The whole place suddenly 'pops' as if some critical mass had been reached. The garden surges into vital action, moving from near desert to lush jungle in a seeming instant, exploding with living energy. Everyone who practices permaculture and ecological gardening for a few years has seen this amazing transformation.[*]

Seven years. There are asparagus, herb and vegetable gardens, sheltered by box hedges. There are berries and crimson cherries that ripen on Christmas Eve. There are fat double-flowering crabapples, like bridesmaids in the spring. There are russet apples, an avocado laden with pears, Moorpark apricots for jam and bottling, and eating standing beneath the tree in the summer twilight.

The hedges are filling in – karaka, wineberry, five-finger, tītoki, bay, kōhūhū, weeping pears – tall mixed hedges, in shades of white and silver and green in honour of the kererū. Everywhere, among the elderberries and scarlet crabapples

---

[*] Toby Hemenway. *Gaia's Garden: A Guide to Home-Scale Permaculture* (White River Junction, VT: Chelsea Green Publishing, 2nd ed., 2009).

that hold their fruit through the winter, there is a tithe of fruit for the birds.

The apprenticeship is done. The adventure of watching it grow begins, as it does every spring.


## VI.

*'I don't know what I will do some future winter, when there is no more room to plant trees.'*

When the last space for trees was filled I left this garden, and Featherston: in the end I was just passing through on the way somewhere else. I left on the winter solstice, as the world turned again towards spring; someone else will watch my garden grow.

## Alice Te Punga Somerville
# Shine Bright Like a Moko:
# The History of Rihanna's Tattoo

This is, at its heart, the story of a single human hand; it is also, across its breadth, the story of race, colonialism, empire, gender and indigeneity. And at its full depth, this is the story of the fine line between cultural appropriation and cultural exchange.

It's the story of a young Caribbean woman of African origins; a citizen of Barbados, a former English colony also claimed at earlier points by Spain and Portugal, from which Indigenous people have been, if not entirely extermi-nated, incorporated and made invisible. This young woman is a musician whose exuberant, plucky, self-assured public persona is the vehicle for a multi-platinum recording career, featuring glamorous live performances of incredibly catchy songs, among them 'Shine Bright Like a Diamond'.

When Rihanna included Auckland in her 2013 Diamonds world tour, a third concert was added to cater to the massive demand for tickets. But what received worldwide publicity was the story of how, while in Aotearoa, she acquired a new tattoo to add to an already impressive collection of body art. The new tattoo, on her right hand, was done tradition-ally (tapping with a chisel, not buzzing with a needle) by a

First published in a longer version on Alice's blog Once Were Pacific, 5 November 2013 (http://oncewerepacific.blogspot.co.nz/2013/11/shine-bright-like-moko-history-of.html).

Māori artist, in the aesthetic form of a design he learned from a Sāmoan master tattoo cultural practitioner, while a Māori singer provided moral support.

For weeks afterwards, Pacific people in Aotearoa, the Pacific region and beyond debated via social media and over cups of tea what the tattoo signified, and whether it was a moko, kiri tuhi, malu, or just a plain old tattoo.

In the meantime, according to later media reports, Rihanna decided she didn't 'love, love' the tattoo anyway, and flew her favourite tattoo artists, a white American man and a young, white British woman, to the Dominican Republic to rework it into a new design, one that allegedly draws its inspiration from traditional henna patterns.

### *You've got to hand it to her: the landscape of a single human hand*

Rihanna's hand is now a landscape; literally it is a contested place, but also metaphorically it is the place where imperial histories play themselves out. Rihanna's hand has become a landscape in the way that Indigenous people know land-scapes: it belongs to someone who has known it as long as it has existed, and while for some people it now represents a resource to be exploited, for others it is a result and continua-tion of complicated and important family histories. She is not the first black woman whose body bears the traces of histo-ries of violence and appropriation; she is not the first woman of African descent whose body is held up for close inspec-tion by 'the world' (see, for example – or refuse to – Sarah Baartman, the Khoikhoi woman from southern Africa who was paraded through nineteenth-century Europe under the name 'Hottentot Venus').

In the field of literary studies, we often talk about the palimpsest, a piece of paper used over and over again so that when you read the latest words applied to its surface, you can't help but be aware of – and even distracted by – the other texts that have existed underneath. The palimpsest I encounter most often in my day to day life is my shopping list scrawled on a piece of paper that turns out (upon closer inspection, while pushing a trolley around the supermarket) to be a bill, a letter or an interesting clipping. We are able to read the surface text for its meaning (I need tomatoes and shampoo) at the same time as we consider the literal meaning of other writings underneath (oh look, the phone bill is $128) as well as the histories – the past lives – of those former texts (wait, did I pay this bill?).

Palimpsests are actual things because of the historical (and in my household anyway, apparently continuing) scarcity of paper or other such materials, but the palimpsest is also a rich and versatile metaphor. It can be helpful to talk about places, for example, as palimpsests. Rather than deciding there is only one possible story for any place, as suggested by maps in which countries have neat borders and cheerfully appear in different and unmodulated colours, the metaphor of the palimpsest reminds us it is impossible to engage with any one account of history (a story about history, or some material proof) without noticing – and even being distracted by – the many layers of history underneath.

Rihanna's hand is a palimpsest because it is a surface on which stories have been layered: at the most basic level, a tattoo, then another tattoo. However, each of those stories is itself another story. The first tattoo is wrapped up in a story of Māori and Sāmoan cultural revitalisation, specifically in the area of applying ink to the body; and the involvement of another Māori person, like Rihanna, a musical artist.

And this story is wrapped up in other stories, each of which is densely packed with still more stories: why cultural revitalisation via tattoo was necessary (which opens up even more stories about the role of Christianity and the literal outlawing of tattoos in the Pacific; and national and regional interruptions in cultural practice as a result of a long history of Europeans understanding Pacific people as savages). There are other stories about the tattooing of women, which invoke a whole range of understandings about gender and the tattoo, from a Sāmoan origin story about twin sisters who swam from Fiji with a specific set of instructions, to the reclaiming of malu and moko by young Polynesian and Māori feminists in 1970s Auckland, and beyond. There are stories about why Māori and Sāmoan people would have such a close relationship in the first place (via New Zealand's colonial history in Sāmoa, through overt as well as economic imperialism). Still more stories. And more. And more.

### She found culture in a hopeless place

The things (tattoos? malu? tatau? moko? kiri tuhi?) applied to Rihanna's hand in Aotearoa piqued such collective interest not because of the aesthetic dimension of the design but because of these stories. The history of Indigenous Pacific control over our own cultural practices, including practices of tattooing and other body arts, is so complicated that we have inevitably overreacted to Rihanna's hand. We first responded to her decision to acquire the tattoo, and a few days later we responded to her decision to (attempt to) cover it up. Such an energetic reaction is understandable, because her decision to acquire such a tattoo in such a context brings up a rollercoaster of emotions: pride, jealousy, defensiveness, anger and shame. We believe we are reacting appropriately (rather than overreacting) because the sheer bulk of past and ongoing injustices and appropriations, weighing heavily as they do on ourselves and also on our descendants, justifies our response.

And Rihanna's tattoos are not in any way an aberration; they follow hot on the heels of the Fiji Airlines decision to legally copyright specific elements of the traditional design of its new logo, and New York designer Nanette Lepore's appropriation of Fijian masi for a tiny dress she labelled 'Aztec'. Closer to home, Air New Zealand defended its rejection of a would-be flight attendant on the grounds that she sported ta moko, supposedly because it might alarm customers – while happily using traditional Māori design in other aspects of its brand, notably the iconic koru on the tails of its airplanes. All of these acts tell stories, and all of them invoke stories. Because so much has been taken, because cultural integrity and cultural proximity are still such flimsy things in 2013 in our region, and because of Rihanna's sheer fame, we respond to this one specific hand-sized situation in ways that feel – that are – important.

After all, this is not really about Rihanna's hand – what power could the small hand of a single Barbadian woman really have over us? It is about the many layers of history we cannot help but see when we look at her skin. And as we 'read' each text, more texts become apparent: her African skin bearing the marks of Caribbean diaspora, the tattoo applied in Aotearoa, and finally a design applied in another (Spanish-speaking) part of the Caribbean, which is apparently intended to look like the henna design which has its roots in the Indian subcontinent. Note, too, that the movement of 'henna design' from its home to the Caribbean comes through at least two pathways. There is the general historical movement of Indian people to plantations in the Caribbean via the British system of indentured labour (which also brought Indian people to Fiji), and the economic migration of people from India to Barbados over the past century. There is also the contemporary appropriation, by the hegemonic American popular culture in which Rihanna and her career are embroiled, of Indian culture (from butter chicken to bindis and henna and so on). These borrowings are removed from the inconvenient truth of India's geographic and cultural proximity to states deemed by the United States as questionable in relation to terrorist activities, but they also quietly pick up on a long history of what Edward Said called 'Orientalism' back in the late 1970s. On some level, then, the conscious decision made by Rihanna to cover the prior 'Pacific' tattoo with a henna-inspired tattoo is one small part of a larger picture of the longstanding link between India and the Caribbean, and the circulation of specific Indigenous cultural forms in the context of European (and American) imperialism.

But once we stand back and see this much bigger picture, how do we think about the person who sparked it? Am I claiming that Rihanna has no agency, that she has no choice, that she is powerless in the face of the broad sweep and devastating waves of colonialism? Do I see her as a thoughtless pawn in someone else's game? Am I replicating the history of non-African people treating African people as if they have the intellectual capacity of children? Am I expecting more from Rihanna because she is one of 'our own'? Is it okay to expect that a person who is rather more from the victim rather than the victor part of the colonial story would use her considerable position of power to make visible the plight of other victims, or at least not replicate the same old systems of cultural appropriation?

*Shine bright like a moko: a tattoo, a beloved grandchild*

This isn't only about Rihanna – this is about us. We have all participated in viewing Rihanna's hand as if it had been removed from the rest of her body, because this is how the photographs have been distributed in corporate and social media. Peering at the layers of ink, we find ourselves concentrating on separating the overlapping patterns, rather than asking questions about the rest of the body to which the hand is attached. Each time we do this, we normalise the chopping up of black women's bodies. We like to think we are outraged by the unauthorised removal of body parts from Indigenous bodies for medical research, but we are happy to visually detach a body part for the purpose of arguments about cultural integrity. It is awkward to realise that we have no problem treating Rihanna's body the way her then-partner Chris Brown did just before those famous photographs of domestic assault: as something upon which to project our own violence; as something in which her body is less valuable than us and our ideas. Even as we stare at the photographs of her hand, making arguments about the importance of cultural wholeness and continuity, we sidestep the rather uncomfortable situation in which the ink on her hand means more to us than the blood that flows in and out of the living heart located somewhere out of the view of the camera. In our single-minded focus on those tattoos, we have chosen our holy liquid: ink is more important to us than blood.

Of course, in te reo Māori we have a little pun on the word 'moko'. As well as meaning 'tattoo' it is widely used as a shortened form of 'mokopuna', or grandchild. Rihanna is a descendent of her own family tree, a family tree that includes a number of branches. We all are. Surely our ancestors not only want us to be alive but they also want us to be well:

physically, emotionally, spiritually, culturally well. I was angry with Rihanna when I started writing this, but now I feel only aroha for her. I wish her all the best. I hope one day she finds a way to shine bright like a moko of her own ancestors, rather than looking for who she is in a palimpsest of other peoples' moko stretched across the skin of her hand.

## David Herkt
# Paul

If you ask, Paul will tell you that when he was born he didn't breathe and it took a long time before he did which is why he has a disability. For a time he seemed to want to tell the story with frequency. It was the beginning of everything. It was what made him different. It was a strange and wondrous event. It needed to be told and repeated.

Paul is intellectually disabled. He doesn't quite know the detail of the bodily responses that were involved, the death of brain cells from oxygen deprivation during birth and the effect this has had on his thoughts, emotions and mobility, but he lives with the consequences: his odd walk which emphasises his right side, his strange stiffness, his learning difficulties, his staring facial expressions, his confusions and his relative lack of emotional control.

He has short self-cut hair which he dyes black, unwilling in his mid-forties to let the grey streaks show. He has brown eyes. He tans easily. He has had all his teeth out and has refused false teeth. He was rejected by his family and he was raised in homes for the intellectually disabled until he decided on self-sufficiency and repeatedly pestered those concerned until finally it happened. I would describe Paul as my friend, but it is much deeper now, after fourteen years, than friendship.

First published on David's blog Notes & Queries, on Public Address, June 2013 (http://publicaddress.net/im%3A8577/paul/).

I talk to him on a daily basis. We discuss weather, shopping, TV, politics, the news, and his neighbours. I see him almost every week. We have bitter fights with regularity, which are frequently loud and unpleasant. Paul is also gay, which leads to some commonality of interest and at times a source of drama, for Paul is nothing if not a drama queen, and his sense of theatre has been honed by endless hours of soap operas on TV or DVD.

How did I meet him?

It was the budgies that did it. I worked for a while establishing a database for a volunteer gay and lesbian telephone counselling service, and because I had also had counselling training from a long time before, I found myself more involved. Paul was a frequent caller. The manager who ran the service regarded him as someone who couldn't 'progress' so Paul got what I regarded as a fairly short shrift – his problems weren't deemed interesting or solvable.

Paul was phoning more out of loneliness than any other issue. I found I liked talking to him, and often did so, but he had budgies and the plight of his birds, as he explained it, unable to really move or stretch their wings in their too-small cage, eventually got to me.

I purchased the largest cage I could afford but I had to ask my partner, John, to deliver it because by the rules of the service I was permitted no 'real-life' contact with our callers. Somehow, at the job's end, when I no longer had to obey the rules, Paul continued on in my life.

Paul lives in a state-provided house in one of Auckland's most deprived areas, a dumping ground for the unloved, unwanted, the crazy and the poor. I had to research the suburb for a TV job once and the statistics are unenviable – number of people on benefits, proximity to liquor outlets, rate of arrest, rate of violent crime. One year, Guy Fawkes coincided with an inorganic rubbish week, and driving through Paul's suburb, the streets piled with discarded household junk outside unloved houses, was like entering a war zone: skyrockets were being fired horizontally across roads, teenagers roamed in gangs, and bunches of crackers sounded like automatic gunfire. It is not somewhere that is going to be in a 100% Pure New Zealand advertisement any time soon.

At the age of three, Paul had been placed in the first of what would become a series of homes for the intellectually disabled. Recently, on his initiative, we revisited one. Now it is partially abandoned. There were bleak bathrooms, wards with stripped-down beds still in place and so crammed together that it was barely possible to move between them, long institutional corridors with lifting carpet, and a dry swimming pool filled with broken furniture.

Paul was eager to see the place in which he had spent his adolescence. The words tumbled out of him. 'This was my ward. My bed was down there. That was where I was raped. That was where I got punched. I used to sit on that step and eat my lunch. A girl went up into that tower and wanted to jump off. They used to wake us at half past six and we'd have a bath. We were very happy here.'

The disjunction between his descriptions and his state of mind was a revelation.

When I first met him, Paul was lonely, unhappy and frustrated, with anger-management problems. He had been arrested and convicted for threatening violence. There were other police visits including the day when a neighbour had complained about him walking outside their house, dressed in women's clothing, with a kitchen knife in hand.

Paul was also being ripped-off financially by a number of

commercial organisations which saw an intellectual disability as something to be exploited. The worst was a TV rent-to-buy company which was still charging him two years after he had paid them off. There was a woman who sold furniture at rates far beyond its valuation. There was the man who offered to take away household goods for inspection and upgrade, and who never returned them. There was also the salesperson for a large communications company who sold Paul an expensive phone plan and a top-of-the-line mobile phone he couldn't afford. They weren't the only ones.

All of these problems required sorting out, complicated by all sorts of weird ethical decisions about the boundaries of Paul's freedom to choose, versus his exploitation – not to mention the boundaries of my own role in things. Gradually I found myself, for better or worse, enmeshed in Paul's life.

I also found Paul intellectually engaging. For example, when I first met him he was obsessed and excited by the whole concept of fiction. He initially thought TV dramas were exactly the same as the news, which was not an uninteresting concept. For Paul, an afternoon soapie was real people's lives. It was real life happening in real time and he wanted to know 'What happens when the TV just goes off them, you know, afterwards?'

Explaining the concept of fiction and acting to him was a revelation. It was intellectually exciting for him. It was a philosophical problem: 'You mean they aren't what they are?' It was thrilling. One saw the splendid lure of fiction played out in someone's mind. I suddenly saw the wonder of saying what was *not*. Being there at Paul's discovery was something that I still value. A huge chunk of human culture came home to me in that instant.

But all this fiction and drama has run-on effects. Once Paul had to be put under anaesthetic for a major dental operation, and I was gowned up to accompany him into the operating theatre as a familiar face to soothe his fears. It was like putting down a Tennessee Williams heroine who had been raised on TV dialogue. Paul was Blanche Dubois at the mercy of strangers: straws were clutched, every word he uttered could have been scripted by an Academy Award team ('You can't just leave me here with these people!') and he swooned perfectly as the anaesthetic hit home.

Paul has given me much to consider, including just how innate is gaydom? Paul is somehow naturally gay. He has never really socialised with gay people, so his personal delicacy, his effeminacy, his preference for purses, the hair dye, and his sense of 'gay drama', have not come from a gay milieu. It seems, in his case, gay came first, before acculturation.

He also has unsuspected talents, like an extreme facility with dates. Paul must be the only person I know who remembers the Prime Minister John Key's birthdate, along with those of the late Paul Holmes, Helen Clark, and his budgies: 'It's my budgie's four and a half year birthday today.' This has a downside – Paul likes things organised weeks, if not months, in advance, something hard to live up to if you deal in lesser schedules. Paul is happily organising events for a date months in the future, which he knows will be a Tuesday.

*

It seemed a simple thing – to provide someone 'differently abled' with a bit of company and be there to sort out problems to which he didn't know the answers – but it turned out to be anything but simple.

There was the $1000 debt to a sex-line company where Paul had utilised his fairly omni-sexual voice to engage in sexual banter with heterosexual callers, who thought they were talking to 'Pauline'. Unfortunately Paul was being charged by the minute. There was the institution of a toll-bar (which Paul still insists on referring to as a 'tow-bar') to prevent further occurrences, which he promptly got around by changing his phone number so that all previous service qualifications were removed. He might be intellectually disabled but he isn't stupid. Another $800 debt he had to pay off to a sex-line company from his benefit seemed to finally cure this problem.

There was also the 'flatmate wanted' ad which Paul ran in a paper that offered free listings. 'Flatmate wanted by gay intellectually disabled man' was an unsuspected source of complications. For Paul it operated as the equivalent of a 'sex-offered' ad which I hadn't realised. It was surprising the number of men who responded and came around to 'look at the room'. 'It was terrible – he had a baby-seat in the back of the car,' Paul said, with a perfect sly delivery, of one brief sexual encounter.

He was reluctant to stop the ad running, and who could blame him? It provided sex, human contact, and drama. But eventually he realised the consequences were sometimes not entirely pleasant. There were his emotions, there were the odd requests (his foray into cross-dressing was a direct result of one ad-respondent's interest), and there was the sheer lack of safety.

Then there is Work & Income New Zealand. Paul is on a benefit due to his medical status. He is also on his third trespass order, which prevents him going into his local WINZ office, something which is a relief. The complications that resulted from WINZ losing files, repeatedly mispaying him, failing to institute changes, not communicating, and being generally incompetent are hard enough for the averagely abled human, but were a source of angered frustration for Paul, and he could only express it by threats.

Paul was generally right about their failures, just as he was right about the money owed to him. Still, I relish his being banned and I would almost recommend it as a strategy to any long-term WINZ client. Anyone who has stood on the wrong side of the counter at Paul's local open-plan WINZ and watched the swanning staffers on the other side would agree that it is an experience that does nothing for mental equilibrium. Being banned means the benefit continues, and the computer flags on the files mean WINZ stays away. Being ignored comes as a great relief.

In addition to these factors there were the more personal ones; primarily, Paul falling dramatically and competitively in love with a friend of mine.

I had introduced them both in person. We had all visited. They had also spoken many times on the telephone. But it went much further than that. For Paul, it was love at first sight and for a couple of years I had to deal with jealousies and dramas ramped up way beyond Mills & Boon levels.

It would finally end when my friend went to work in Sydney. Paul decided, without prior arrangement, to go to the airport to see him off. He was accompanied by a torn out *Listener* photograph of the person he was seeking, which he showed to security guards and coffee bar staff. It was heart-rending.

I treat Paul as much as possible the way I'd treat anyone. I demand the same care from him as I would demand from anyone else. It isn't a sensitive new-agey type friendship. I figure a good fight is as valuable a part of a relationship as anything, so we argue often, and as equals. I remind him to care for his budgies properly ('Have you given them some greens?') and he fibs about whether he has done his cleaning or not.

You do have to be aware of just who Paul is, and there is always his frustration of quite literally being exiled from ordinary life and being alert enough to realise it. He also does not deal with change easily. You can't alter a plan with Paul without a huge fuss. A time is a time and a scheduled date is a scheduled date. But somehow no matter how annoyed you might get with him (frequently I've had to delete forty-odd nasty voicemail messages) and how abusive he might have been to you ('You little shit, I'm going to kill you'), you have to pull back a little and see things as they are.

When Paul is abusive, you can almost invariably hear what has been said to him in playback. Sometimes it isn't pleasant to hear the voices of one's fellow beings in Paul's words and locutions. It is the things that have been done to him that you are getting done to you. It is the words that have been shouted at him, that are being shouted at you.

A couple of weeks ago John and I picked up Paul to go to a beach. En route, Paul, who was in a grumpy mood anyway, decided the Titirangi hills were making him car sick and had an attack of Blanche Dubois again. He was faint. He was dizzy. He fanned his face. 'Can't you see I'm very, very ill.' We had to abort the planned trip and no amount of logic or stopping the car for a rest would dissuade Paul from this course of action.

I was annoyed, but when we neared Paul's home, John suggested going down to the nearby Otuataua Stonefields beach to eat our picnic lunch instead. 'Damn you, you little bastard,' Paul said grumpily, while adding 'yes' in a grudging undertone.

That simple hour at a not particularly attractive Manukau Harbour beach remains a really pleasant memory. The tide was full and covered the warm mud flats. A few rounded cumulus clouds were suspended in mid-air. The scrubby unprepossessing shore was deserted except for a few Pacific Islanders flounder-fishing at the far end. The sea and the hills across the Manukau looked just like that 1956 Colin McCahon painting *French Bay,* layered in fractured horizontals of white and blue. Small fish leapt audibly in the shining water.

I sprawled on a rug while John and Paul paddled in the water. Paul was laughing and chatting, the Titirangi drama forgotten now, John was generally agreeing, and as they waded out of earshot and the sense of their words was lost, what I recall is the happy contentment in their voices, the relaxation and trust, the sound of the slight waves, and every-one's small plain pleasure in a shared human instant.

## Gregory Kan
## Borrowed Lungs

In 2001, my parents cobbled together $75,000 that simultaneously allowed our migration to New Zealand, and would eventually bond me to two years of National Service in Singapore. Six years later, when the time came, there was no outward trace of it. No government-officiated letter or phone call reached the house in Saint Johns where I lived with my parents. My friends in Auckland knew I was about to leave, although it must have been difficult for them to understand its conditions. Some remarked on the impossibility of the decision I'd made. There was no decision, but rather a play of forces – political, economic, legal.

In Singapore, it is compulsory for males who have reached eighteen years of age to enrol in National Service. The term is twenty-two or twenty-four months, depending on one's physical fitness on enrolment. I was to serve in the armed forces, as part of its conscripted military, for twenty-four months. My family paid a bond because we wished to live elsewhere; but I was deemed to have lived in Singapore long enough to have to return. Refusal entailed a summary trial or court martial in the military justice system, on charge of being AWOL. In short, I would be arrested if I ever landed at Changi airport – even in transit. My return was a ventriloquism emergent of a force-field, an inexorable cultural

First published in *The Pantograph Punch*, 3 May 2013
(http://pantograph-punch.com/borrowed-lungs-my-life-as-a-conscript).

response and not a decision. Around the end of the last year of my Auckland high-school education, I packed my suitcase, boarded a plane, and was given my first real lesson in power.

*

In nine strokes, beginning from my right temple, I no longer had hair. I was moved from the large room we'd started in to another large room of shaven heads. I found myself unable to recognise anyone I'd met in the first. We put on grey training singlets. We were told how to arrange the items in our lockers for inspections. Fifteen strangers slept in one room that night. I thought that we all had the same face, that we all had the same eyes.

As recruits during the first three months of service, we were told where to go and what to do (i.e. herded) by section instructors, who bore a sergeant rank. Their orders were legitimised by commissioned officers – the 'fathers' above our non-commissioned 'mothers'. Intensity plays a fundamental role in the formation of memory. As with childhood, I remember the ways we were punished more easily than the ways we were actually trained.

Sometimes, in seemingly arbitrary fashion, we were given impossible timings to meet. 'Change Parade', for example, would proceed as follows: thirty people stampede back upstairs, to fall-in again in completely different gears. You're late. Change into your Smart-4 (neatly folded and pressed camouflage fatigues and parade boots). Your ten minutes started six minutes ago. You're late. Change into your PT kit (singlet, running shorts and shoes). You're late. Change into your admin attire . . . and so on.

Against the already overwhelming tropical heat and humidity, some would risk donning their camouflage fatigues over their singlets, trying to save seconds. Others would arrive downstairs in the entirely wrong attire. And so on. I would arrive downstairs to find the rest of the platoon already neatly arranged – 45 degrees to the left, in push-up position.

For failing bunk inspections, we were banned from sleeping on our beds during the day, so that we were forced to preserve the cleanliness of the floors if we wanted to nap. In our first extended period of training in the jungle, we performed back-crawls, rifles held above our chests, through our latrine area. The final day of the twenty-two or twenty-four months of National Service is called 'ORD' or Operational Readiness Day. I never once in the army considered my operational readiness. I don't think many of us did. I just wanted to get through.

In basic training I attracted the term '*jiak kan tang*', or *kan tang* for short, which roughly translates as 'potato eater'. While on its surface the designation was a mockery of my Anglophone accent, the act of distancing ran deeper. My section instructor once told me that I was arrogant, and that I felt I was better than the others, even though I constantly felt frail and incapable. At the time I didn't realise that my accent bore class significations, as well as cultural ones. I did come from an upper middle-class background, although my family lost most of its money during the 1997 Asian Financial Crisis. And we did have enough money to move to New Zealand. Yet while I felt different – certainly after discovering the way I spoke was conflated by the others with dietary habit – I never felt better than the others. I was often clumsy. I was always dazed. It took me a while to grasp lessons, especially when I was running around with the dual weights of helmet and rifle. (And it was true what instructors said – you were dumber the instant you put on a helmet.) So the prejudice confused me, and while it largely fell away among the other recruits as they got to know me better, my section instructor persisted in his. Shaking his head – after witnessing a particularly mazy run of mine through the underbrush that probably would have guaranteed my annihilation by friendly fire in real combat conditions – he told me that 'someone like you will never get this'. It was difficult to feel foreign in Singapore as well as New Zealand. And it was difficult to find Singapore a more foreign place than New Zealand.

Filling out an expression-of-interest form at the end of basic training (which lasted three months), I marked 'Yes' to be considered for command school. There were a number of reasons to compete for a place in officer cadet school (the 'higher' of two possibilities for the remainder of my service – the other was a place in a course to become a non-commissioned officer). Commissioned officers received twice as much by way of allowance. They had better food at the officers' mess, and cheap beer. They had proper rooms and bathrooms. And commissioned officers were the ones who had power over the others.

It is obvious to me now that this was the moment where I decided to gain the most power to guarantee the most protection. It wasn't so much one particular event – say, the time I watched someone forced to run around a building yelling 'I am a stupid bird!' over and over, or any other senseless dehumanisation in the name of regimentation I may have experienced – but rather the knowledge that I could be subject to such an event at any given time, for any reason, real or contrived. In general, I wanted to escape. By this point my otherness had also become firmly ingrained in my psyche; I thought that perhaps by joining the command structure I could transcend my difference.

I got to officer cadet school, eventually, after being funnelled through a regime of assessments measuring my physical fitness, combat fitness, command and control, emotional stability and tactical awareness and knowledge. The officer cadet course was a nine-month extension of this. I remember trying to decide where to send my machine-gun team while my instructor struck me repeatedly in the helmet and screamed at me. I laughed a lot in these times. Short, sharp bursts – not in amusement, but to expel the moment's sheer excess. Crying wouldn't have been quick enough.

*

Beside a large river in Brunei, I tore the head off a quail, as instructed. I was on an eleven-day jungle confidence course, one of the more brutal moments of officer cadet school. The bird's liver was reddish-brown with no white spots, which meant the quail should have been healthy enough to eat, but I threw it into the river as soon as the instructors left on their boats. The smell of blood on my hands stayed for days. The first sound of rain reaching the jungle canopy was always far enough away for me to hope it was the wind. I heard later that one of my platoon mates had lost his machete in the rising mud. In the jungle I came to know a darkness full of noise, none of which I could recognise.

It had been four or five months since my commissioning. An officer is recognised by the display of rank on the shoulder, instead of on the arm. I grew accustomed to soldiers falling silent when I passed them in hallways, or in forests, on parade grounds, or in offices. You can follow the trajectory of a body as it passes through one knot of forces to the next. In gaining rank, I had not been given power, I had been given over to power. With each successive command I issued, I realised that I was nowhere nearer to claiming individual expression, let alone control. I became aware of myself as a mere body positioned to channel an imperative from a larger, regularising network of forces. It was agency, but it was an impersonal agency. For the moment, it had borrowed a pair of lips.

Part of the reconnaissance course we conducted involved resistance-to-interrogation training. The trainees were captured. Their weapons and equipment were taken away. They were cable-tied and blindfolded. The blindfolds had numbers on them. The trainees were addressed from then on by the number on the blindfold. They were gathered in a single area bounded by concertina wire. They were placed in high-stress positions which involved various kneels and squats, whose specifically inventive contortions ensured a significant intensification of pain over the ten or twelve hours they were forced to hold them. Many of the trainees fell asleep in these positions, having already been carrying out missions for the past three or four days. They were jarred awake by instructions to change position screamed at them through a loud-hailer. Individuals were led to rooms where their blindfolds were removed and they were interrogated over maps for information. I have been on both sides of the blindfold. I have never seen so many bodies contained and processed this way.

I remember that when I was in primary school, there were pencil sharpeners that could be bought cheaply from the school stationery store. These had a small plastic container attached that held pencil shavings. Most of us used these containers to house our spiders. I had a glass jar with a magnifying lid to keep mine in. The spiders we found were all more or less the same size, and I always thought they had the same face. The original intention was for them to fight and kill each other, but we struggled just to keep them alive. Even when we managed to put two of them together they often seemed uninterested in fighting. Made faceless, individual differences erased, reduced to bodies, further reduced to body parts (trigger-hand, aiming-eye, crouching-legs), all for easy manipulation and mobilisation in a theatre of war.

One day after receiving my civilian papers and walking out of camp with my gear bag for the last time, I was back in New Zealand and back in school. It was already the second week of semester. Was it weird to find myself sitting beside fresh-faced eighteen-year-olds in a lecture theatre at Auckland University, hours later and half a world away? Not as weird as I expected. The university is also a processing centre for bodies, to prepare them for the theatre of work. I sat with about four hundred others, neatly arranged in a lecture hall often jokingly referred to as 'The Fridge'.

I wish I were better able, at this point in my life, to trace the changes that followed me out of the army into my civilian life. Most of those are still indeterminate, and require further dragging through the mush and opacity of experience. But there are little strangenesses. When walking down a dirt track at night I am sometimes confused about which country I'm in. All dirt tracks feel the same to me, at night. I like leaving rooms more than I do entering them. I am never late, unless I want to be. I feel safe in forests, whose chaotic ecologies of overcoming and displacement elude all apparatus of capture.

# Allan Smith
## What I learned from Momo: or, When is a house a stand of trees?

*I wanted simply to return to the scene of my childhood,
ultimately with the feeling that what we can achieve in life
is little other than the attempt to recapture our childhood in
different form.* – Theodor Adorno, explaining why he returned
to Germany after 1945

I don't think I'll ever be done with revisiting childhood memories of living in a two-storey wooden house designed and built by my uncle, Maurice K. Smith – or Momo as he was to us then – for my parents in Glen Eden. I lived in that house from the age of one year and eleven months, until I was six years and eleven months. A few years ago, I was sent a set of digital images of the house, based on slides taken by my uncle in the early 1950s when it was under construction. With their muted colourations of framework and cladding, coarse grass, and macrocarpa pines, these images – which I never knew existed until then – seemed to spring directly from the shadows of my own memory bank. The aroma of the house's timber and the sound of its cracking in a double height of

First published in longer form in A. Smith and L. Tweedie-Cullen (eds), *distracted-reader #1: Mixtures: Xin Cheng and Allan Smith* (split/fountain, Auckland, 2013, www.splitfountain.org/?p=6871). The epigraph by Adorno is from Stefan Müller-Doohm, trans. Rodney Livingstone, *Adorno: A Biography* (Cambridge UK: Polity Press, 2005), p. 25.

dust, sun, and shade were immediately relayed through the prism of those photographs.*

I slept upstairs on the landing between my parents' and big sisters' rooms, under the steeply sloping roof with its exposed Oregon beams. Just across from my bed, next to a small window where the roof almost met the floor, there was a large, dusty scale model made from square-section balsa strip and pins. This was the original maquette for the geodesic dome Maurice designed and had built on the fields of Western Springs at very short notice for the Auckland City Council's Birthday Carnival in 1956. The dome, sheathed in plywood and coloured fibreglass panels, was based on Buckminster Fuller's first American geodesic dome and his principles of 'synergetic geometry'.

Although most of the variation and differentiation of the Glen Eden house was on the inside – a built constellation inside a perforated, barn-like shell – it primed me to anticipate nested and ramified spaces in the wider world. The house's language of materials and construction taught me something about how to get purchase on the world and how to move through it and amongst it. Much of what I want from architectural and landscape spaces has been substantially shaped by my few years in that house.

*

When I was five years old, a small group of teachers made a point of showing me that every day during writing and

---

\*    These images can now be found on the digitised MIT Libraries Collection website, Dome: http://dome.mit.edu/handle/1721.3/47998. Search under Glen Eden, or Bryan Smith house.

drawing time I would only ever pick the card saying 'This is a ____' as a prompt for what to draw; which usually in my case was a fire engine. The more advanced children in my class were choosing phrases like 'This is Mummy and me going to the ____', or 'Here we are making ____.' In other words, I was finding it difficult to make transitions between the intransitive and transitive modes of experience; to move from isolated objects to relations between things.

Modern art and architecture often draw their energy from squaring off intensely concrete particulars against collective rhythms of organisation. The Glen Eden house and other works by Maurice that made an early impression on me are all about putting things together; about getting from here to there concretely, through measured and accented transitions. They are, if you like, about how to constantly move between conditions of the intransitive and the transitive; about recognising connections between one thing and many others; between stationary objects and mobile groups of things. I eventually came to recognise a convenient convergence between the additive and collaging modes of modernism and my own ways of adjusting to a disjunctive and disorientating world.

Among the things Maurice left behind when he moved permanently to the States in 1958 were a few objects that began to intrigue me during my teenage years – and by then I had also developed a proprietorial fascination for some images of Maurice's early work in Massachusetts. Together, these talismanic fragments provided links to an absent uncle, but they were tantalisingly incomplete. They included:

A box of tiles left over from the mural he designed for the Odeon Theatre in Auckland's Queen Street.
A small hexagonal wooden plug – one of many tapered to fit and

link the struts of the carnival dome.
A wooden puzzle box, whose secret I never discovered.
A partially damaged panel, with Perspex rectangles and squares
projecting from its red, black, white, brown and gold surface.
Slides my father took of Maurice's Cleaves Hill Road house in
Harvard, Massachusetts, surrounded by snow and trees.
Black and white photographs in a 1967 *Harvard Review*
magazine of a house Maurice designed in Groton, MA.

Maurice had annotated the *Harvard Review* images with lines
from Lewis Carroll's *Through the Looking Glass*. As I became
more consciously interested in such things, I came to think of
Maurice as a maker of puzzle-like objects; a Magister Ludi
of syncopated surfaces and three-dimensional board games.
He was someone who presided over faceted worlds of glass,
timber, and colour. My abiding sense of his houses is of plat-
forms and rooms among trees; spars and masts outside the
house with trunks and branches parcelling out spaces inside.

*

I made my first visit to the Cleaves Hill Road home, set
among tall trees in rural Massachusetts, during the Christmas
of 1985. Via conversations and slide shows with Maurice
I was inducted into the intricate differentiations of 'form
language'; of ways to parse the rich complexities of structure
and material in the physical world, whether built or natural.
Books and writers were recommended – well-stocked larders
of language, pictures, and objects – which included:

A George Herriman *Krazy Kat* compendium.
Christian Norberg-Schulz's *Genius Loci: Towards a*

*Phenomenology of Architecture.*
Bernard Rudofsky's *Architecture Without Architects.*
Primo Levi's *The Wrench.*
Michel Tournier's *The Four Wise Men.*
Francis Ponge's *Things.*

From an array of texts and terminologies, colours and textures, a slide Maurice showed me of a circular collage stood
out. (On my last trip, in May 2012, the actual collage was
there, wedged between timber trim and kitchen clutter, with
an assortment of tiny toy creatures and decorative beads
hanging off it.) The collage was one of several Maurice had
made as birthday cards for friends and family. My father had
been sent a square one that was like an inorganic hoarfrost; a
delicate sprinkle of shiny bits on metal foil, which had been
stapled to a small piece of plywood. The circular one – a great
deal more intense than my father's birthday collage – has
obsessed me for years.

This particular collage is many things. On an inch-
thick disc of medium-density fibre board about one foot in
diameter with its skin of metallic sheet, the game begins.
Eight splayed strips of varying lengths of the same foil-
faced MDF displace the surface upwards by an inch. Each
of the strips has a squared-off end inside the circle and
a curved one matching its outside edge. Two square foil-
skimmed blocks don't stand as proud as the sectioned
strips, but are tilted diamond-wise toward them. Deployed
on this tabletop topography are plastic electrical connec-
tors, fine brass sleeves like tiny turned candlesticks, slender
metal pipes with on/off crimping, nails, a glass counter like
a transparent backgammon piece on its side, and short dark
strips of perforated shim metal spacers on long-headed

pushpins. The convergence of countable elements plays out a slow-motion explosion of scintillant parts, animated by alliterative stutter. The collage is a collision of light-industrial coruscations. It's a dense-packed array of ranks in unison with switchback glare. It's what American poet Clark Coolidge would call 'a sort of very bright cam'.*

The disc's mineral glitter of staggered phalanxes in careful drill is switchboard information and optical braille. It's the criss-cross of an industrial light display. It's a multi-mirrored monad made from off-cuts that concentrates then spins its luxurious gravel outward; like a carpenter's model of Borges' Aleph seen under the stairs. It's a silver dollar slab of materialist intrigue; a weirdly spoked wheel from Ezekiel's bicycle. Sheeny breakfast tray with linear fretting, Maurice's disc-world answers Paul Simon's simile that maps the sinuous gleam of the Mississippi on the metal of some National guitar.

Freighted with cravings for weighted particulars, the disc collage reminds me of palaeontologist and priest Teilhard de Chardin remembering his childhood fixation on the hexagonal head of a metal bolt, 'which protruded above the level of the nursery floor'. When Teilhard was young, he looked for objects – or part-objects like the metal bolt – of maximal material concentration, of 'sharply individualized' plenitude. He says that during those years a fragment of metal could contain and concentrate for him 'an intensity of resonance and a whole stream of demands' of which his entire spiritual life since then had been 'no more than the development'.†

---

* Clark Coolidge, 'A Note on Bop', in *Now It's Jazz: Writings on Kerouac and the Sounds* (Albuquerque, New Mexico: Living Batch Press, 1999), p. 95.
† Pierre Teilhard de Chardin, *The Heart of Matter*, trans. René Hague (San Diego, CA: Harcourt, 1978), p. 18.

There is also a family resemblance between Maurice's disc collage, and the plywood discs on stubby dowels that his mother (my Nanna) used for the tiered cakes she decorated so elaborately. As long as he didn't chatter, young Maurice was allowed to watch for hours on a stool in the bay window of the front room as Nanna worked on the cakes. Much of what Nanna was putting time and energy into was the piping of all the delicate 'trellises, virtual greenhouses, leaves and roses, etc., . . . half of which were in the space *outside* the cake!'* Maurice also recalls watching his accountant father write a very neat hand in his office ledgers, and retains vivid memories of him 'sawing bread' on the family bread board at home (another tabletop disc – this one with octagonal facets). Sawing, and then shepherding lines of crumbs around the board with the bread knife. If the crumbs went off the board they were brought back. And without talking, his father would do this for long periods of time: 'doing it and looking at it and thinking about something else; blocking any exchange'.

Both decorated cake and bread board have a relationship with what lies outside their perimeters; both objects have partially permeable edges. During the years he taught at MIT, Maurice often added a Gertrude Stein quote to his collaged class hand-outs – a favourite one referred to a painting's dialogue with its physical and ontological neighbourhood:

> I have thought a great deal about all this and I am still thinking about it. I have passionately hoped that some picture would remain out of its frame, I think it can even while it does not, even

---

\* All quoted comments from Maurice are from notes taken in either December 1985 or May 2012.

> while it remains there. . . . the first hope of a painter . . . is the hope
> that the painting will move, that it will live outside its frame.[*]

Maurice recalls a visit to Ian Athfield in his own house over-looking Wellington harbour in 1968 – and Athfield leaning a large old picture frame near a window to whimsically parody conventions of framing and fixed viewpoints.

In a similar vein, he relays a story New Zealand land-scape designer Harry Turbott told him about living with the American landscape architect Dan Kiley on the shores of Lake Champlain in Vermont in the late 1950s, and of the Kileys' eight children, 'living wild like an independent tribe'. Kiley once got his children to help him with tree placement for a project by giving each one a rubber or metal stamp with a dif-ferent tree on it, then telling them to bang their stamps down wherever they chose across a large sheet of paper until told to stop. The different tree types were mixed and dispersed in a way that avoided any of the tired symmetries of classical, beaux-arts garden planning: Kiley was 'looking for actions that didn't look contrived'.

In almost every way, Maurice's approach to formal or-ganisation, and to architecture's rapport with the unframed collage-fields of the world, is in sharp contrast to the ration-alist diagram of the modernist International Style. Too often, modern architecture has focused on creating beautiful isolate objects, immaculate singularities, or dealing with large-scale contexts through uninflected repetition and modularity. There is a shared, stilted isolationism in the phrases 'This is a

---

[*]  Gertrude Stein, quoted in Maurice K. Smith, 'Not-Writing on Built Form',
    *Harvard Educational Review, Architecture and Education*, vol. 39, no. 4, 1969,
    p. 70.

fire engine' and 'This is the Villa Savoye'. The concept of the
field organisation, however, crucial to Maurice's thinking and
making, is all about associative continuities that grow as decisions happen on the spot, in context – responsive to material
and structural possibility – not pre-determined by an inflex-
ible plan.

It may sound oxymoronic, but with expansive irony Maurice
even suggests there should be an anti-singularity branch to
the government. Singularities are non-associative; they do
not breed exchanges, reciprocities, or lateral, additive growth
formations. Whereas a great deal of modern architecture
seals itself off from rich thickets of context, Maurice believes
architecture's task is to elaborate and intensify what the surrounding landscape is already doing. At table scale, a collage or
one of Nanna's decorated cakes are examples of what Maurice
calls 'surface-intensification'. They 'intensify something that is
already defined', rather than just decorating a vacant surface.
A collage, then, is a rehearsal for architecture, and architecture is landscape intensification – an assemblage of relations
between building and place – not singular objects on blank
slates.

*

A local example of Maurice's multi-part relationality is
the Odeon Theatre mosaic he designed and completed in
1957–58, just across Queen Street from the Civic Theatre.
Though a little grimy and timeworn, and partially hidden
behind the alterations of an internet café, the mosaic survives
as a mesh of gridded iridescence. My encomium to the disc
collage aside, for Maurice, the circular form was limited – it
lacked the capacity to interlock in the way straight-edged

geometric shapes can. The Odeon mural is a syncopated field of such interlockings, in which tesserae components like polyominoes, or rectilinear letter forms – Ts, Is, Hs, Es, Cs, Ys, Us – constantly repeat, reverse, mirror, and translate themselves at different sizes and at different depths of relief. Maurice thought of the mosaic's contrapuntal layout as being inhabited by candelabra-like shapes moving in their spatial field as animals in a zoo. He intended it all to be readable as a 'collection of stuff which was acrobating itself into the space' like circus performers.

When architects, artists or writers pursue a language of material improvisation, it often develops a whimsical, sportive aspect. Improvisational momentum can appear as a restless, tumbling pursuit of variation and formal play, which nevertheless remains highly deliberated. Friend and mentor György Kepes once observed that Maurice's architectural language was 'nervous'. Kepes meant that everything seems to keep going, pausing rather than literally stopping anywhere. Lintels over doors or windows often continue further on one side than the other, for instance; and at shelf, deck, and building-size we find always a jointing system with pronounced overlaps. Accenting changes of level, use, and direction, the overlaps provide runs and partial staircasings of material. This simultaneous stepping and inflecting of many elements reads as calibrated exhilaration; as material organisation understood as continuous action and response. Part to part accents and sideways shifts create percussive rapport. Metonymic linking and rhythmic excitement drive spacing and displacement.

The stepping and accenting are ways of spelling or counting out the augmenting levels of relations between parts. It's a form of alliteration. It feels a necessary response to the milling plenitude of a world that clamours to be accounted for. In a 1969 text in which multi-form design is contrasted to closure and reduction, Maurice drops in the alliterative line 'the monstrous marching module mechanically menacing all the months'.* The allure of alliteration is insistent when you want to run a stick along the railings of the real; if you want to play the accordion of the world through braille textures and alternations; if you want to feel things click by on the tongue as a ticket-collector of facts.

Clark Coolidge said when he reads Jack Kerouac's prose he can always 'hear the individual words with an intense phys-icality of separation' – that's a good analogy for mosaic's bit by bit accumulation of thousands of tiny, hard pieces and their distribution, seen and felt at speed.† With each tile marking a touch and a join, a patchwork field of modulated incident accrues; a myriad of disconnections builds continuity. A 'step-generated' array of partial self-similarities forms a tes-sellated collective. The constant up and across of countable elements weaves a ceramic textile; a dense fabric of chromatic matter. A glittering field of built light.

\*

If I could meet again those solicitous primary school teachers concerned for my ontological welfare, I would reassure them I have learned something over the years. Just as Teilhard de Chardin moved from his fixation on isolate intensities to a vision of complex cosmic interdependence, I too am always on the lookout for modes of relation between things. I recog-nise that a stand of pines is much more interesting than an

---

* Ibid., p. 69.
† Coolidge, 'Kerouac: A Talk', *Now It's Jazz*, p. 47.

immaculately finished art object enclosed on itself. Although
. . . a fire engine encrusted with equipment, with its packed
metal cupboards and telescoped ladders, and carrying a small
cadre of operators from one place to another to deal with an
elemental breakout of cause and effect – really is a dazzling
sort of thing in its own right.

*Maurice K. Smith (b. 1926 ) graduated from Auckland School
of Architecture in 1950 and left on a Fulbright Scholarship
to the United States where he taught in Kansas for a short
time before enrolling in the architecture program at MIT
for 1952–53. While studying and travelling in the States at
this time he met Frank Lloyd Wright, Rudolph Schindler,
Richard Neutra, György Kepes, Carl Koch and Pietro
Belluschi; worked on Buckminster Fuller's first American
geodesic dome; and was an assistant to Serge Chermayeff.
After returning to work in New Zealand for a few years,
he went back to the States in 1958 to take up a teaching
position in MIT's School of Architecture, which he held
for thirty-four years before retiring in 1996 as emeritus
professor. On sabbatical from MIT he taught for one term
at the Auckland school in 1968. Maurice's built projects and
theoretical texts have appeared in* Spazio e Societa/Space
and Society, Progressive Architecture, Harvard Educational
Review *and* Places.

# Jemima Diki Sherpa
## Three Springs

When there are gatherings in our valley, the women sit with the women and the men sit with the men, and the children tear about evading adult arms that reach out to obstruct their fun. The men form a long line on low benches along the front wall of the house, patriarchs sitting at the end closest to the fire-place with the wide-legged weariness of ageing masculinity, down through the established householders with their roars of laughter, past the young fathers bouncing sticky toddlers on their laps, through the self-conscious new and prospec-tive grooms, to the awkward youths who cram together and snicker and mutter and jostle each other.

Everyone wears down jackets.

In such a line as this, a gambler would have good odds that any man, picked at random, has stood atop of Everest; chances better still that he has been partway up the mountain a dozen times only to return to Base Camp, collect another load, and head off to cross the treacherous icefall again. What elsewhere is extraordinary – the raw material that can be spun into charitable foundations, movie rights, pub boasts and motivational speaking tours – is quotidian in the villages of Thame Valley. Even our monks shed their deep-red robes in spring and come back snow-burnt, the marks of sun goggles

First published on Jemima's blog whathasgood, 23 April 2014 (http://whathasgood.com/2014/04/23/three-springs/).

etched pale across their cheekbones and their lips chapped flaking white with bleeding crimson cracks.

*

When I finished high school and left Kathmandu for university in New Zealand, where my mother is from, I was conditioned for the reactions my last name would elicit. 'They ask how many kilos you can carry,' says every Sherpa who has ever travelled abroad. But I was caught by a more common response: 'Shuuurpa,' in the muted antipodean accent, 'Seriously? That's AWESOME!'

It is something to behold, the open-hearted enthusiasm that the Sherpa name elicits in the western mind. It is (as every random company that has capitalised on it well knows) the branding motherlode – stimulating a vague positive association founded on six-odd decades of mountaineering myth building. I wondered what deep, subconscious connections, what snippets of information, what flashes of imagery were being evoked.

'Awesome' how? I came to ask myself. More importantly, 'awesome' for *whom?* Uncharitably, I imagined them imagining themselves as conquering heroes, assisted by a legion of Sherpa faithful ready – and cheerful – to lay down sweat and lives in service for arduous, but ultimately noble and glorious, personal successes. Still, it is undeniable that, in so-called 'post'-colonial democracies where ethnic minorities carry the burden of insidious and vicious prejudices at every turn, Sherpas are fortunate. Everyone loves us, everyone trusts us, and everyone wants their own collectible one of us. Internet listicles call us 'badass' and we have a very large, very coveted piece of real estate in our back yard. It is a stereotype, sure, but a *positive* one.

Any vague hopes my new acquaintances may have had of me selflessly and single-handedly lugging their furniture upstairs on moving days were swiftly dashed. I lived life some, and then meandered my way home more than half a decade later. Village-born though I was, and potato farmers and yak herders though my grandparents may have been, despite the yearly trips to the Khumbu homeland I am a Kathmandu city girl. Like post-arts-degree twentysomethings the world over, I was adrift. With equal parts defeat, hope, terror, self-congratulation and wildly under-informed plans and good intentions, I arrived 'home' to live in Thamo, elevation: 3550 metres, population: maybe fifty people on a good day.

Village life. This should be amusing.

That was spring 2012, on the first of the Nepali year. It seemed a fitting day for a new chapter.

Two weeks later, a first cousin died on Everest.

Family circumstances were such that I hadn't seen him since we were both infants. My father and another cousin walked to Tengboche to attend the funeral. Grimfaced, they returned. He had a wife and a three-month-old baby, and the then-standard five lakh (roughly US$5000) payout for fatalities would not extend far past the death rites.

Morbidly, perhaps, I read a surprisingly long article on his death. His safety harness had not been clipped in; veteran western (and *only* western) climbers quoted by the half-dozen on the topic of Namgya's death. Overconfidence, the implication was, even though the quote hedged, 'I wouldn't say it's because they are overconfident.' *Strong Sherpa competitive spirit, intra-village rivalries.* 'A bit complacent.' *Sometimes novices just plain forget.* 'These guys just pretty much dance across the ladders.'

This was my first adult experience of the endless, repeating nature of death talk during the spring season. So-and-so, from village such-and-such, his cousin – no, married to her sister, my aunt's – it happened like this. He was such a good person. They say he fell into a crevasse. *Om mani padme hum*.

And then: 'These boys, they go too fast. They hurry to get more work.'

For a lifetime of mountaineering talk, I'd always tuned out. Nuptse and Lhotse get mixed up in my head, and I can never remember the elevations of things, or how many acclimatisation nights there are before a summit, and every climbing company has a name that sounds the same – Adventure something, Mountain something.

But here was how it connected to life, to the cousin I barely knew, to other relatives I knew better who were still on the mountain. As a young high-altitude expedition worker, the more you carry, the more you are paid. There is a per kilogram equation for payment, and there is value, both in hard cash and in securing future work, in proving you are good. If you prove you're good, you get hired next season, possibly recruited by one of the better companies, climbing literally up the mountain and figuratively up the ranks. The best way to do all this is to move fast and carry a lot. And the best way to do *that* is to dance, possibly unclipped, across the icefall ladders.

And yet. This one potential factor, this one whisper of motivation, was something the veteran mountaineers never mentioned when the article posed the question: 'Why did Namgya skip a seemingly simple, and potentially life-saving, step?'

So it *must* have been that Sherpa competitive spirit.

✴

Spring finishes. The potatoes have been planted. The summer fog rolls in, and Thamserku disappears into the mist for days on end. Summer finishes. In autumn I prove I am an exceedingly incompetent dilettante potato harvester. I have better luck interviewing people for an academic study; in a Namche coffee shop, I approach a foreign climbing guide. He pretends to be cagey and worried about his name getting out there. I read him the consent form. Anonymity. You'll really just be a data point, I say curtly, and he looks a bit crushed. He rambles and makes grand pronouncements on how things should be run if anyone was thinking properly. Question 8.1, how satisfied are you in your job. Very satisfied. Question 8.4, do you have plans besides guiding in the future. Maybe write a book about my experiences, he says. The Nepali guides I've asked repeat: *Khai, tyeti bela nai bichar garnu parcha.* Or *Ke garne, aru bikalpa nai chaina.* Question 8.3, *Ajai kati barsa samma yo guiding kaam garnu huncha hola. Aba jati barsa samma jiu le saath dincha bhanumn na, bahini.*

Autumn finishes, and the winds grow colder. Mid-December we descend to Kathmandu. We aren't the only ones; people have trickled down from all the mountain areas, flowing into a river that swirls and swirls clockwise around Boudha in the winter sun.

Spring again, and a friend from university arrives with her boyfriend. I introduce them to khukuri rum, and the next day of collecting tickets and packing for the mountains aches by for all of us. The air in Lukla is crisp, and we set off, arriving home at Thamo the next day. I open up the house, and it is eerily undisturbed despite my aunt's visits over winter. My visitors have plenty of time and a trip to Gokyo won't fill it all, so for days we sit around and read books and make coffee and listen to Kiwi reggae.

I'm bringing in some laundry when my cellphone rings. It's a friend from Kathmandu who works for an international news bureau – there's been a fight, have you heard, who do you know at Base Camp.

The internet has gone mad. Links upon links, hundreds of comments, this one said, then he said, then he said, accusations, counter-accusations, updates, debates, threats, tantrums, analysis, They, Us. I read and I read.

Two aunts and a woman I don't know are weeding a field below ours. I go down and sit with them, and they take a break for tea out of a Thermos and a huge pot of boiled potatoes, peeled with grit-stained hands and dipped in salt and chilli powder from a plastic bag. Did you hear about some fight? I ask, and they haven't. But an icefall doctor has died, originally from down in Solu, but married to so-and-so in her village, two daughters, *nyingje* . . .

My friends and I leave for Gokyo. I carry a pack of cards and along the trail I teach them how to play Callbreak, nabbing guides and porters to come and be our fourth player. Only a couple of hands in, at a tiny lodge in Dole, the game is somehow taken over by trekking guides and I am left keeping score. It becomes a high-stakes game of champions – expert card counters with perfect dramatics. 'On a king of hearts, and my . . . three of spades. *La kha ta.*' Uproar. The round finishes, and as the cards are shuffled some go out to take a leak. I ask – hey, this fight. The foreigners are pissed off apparently, have you heard . . . ? Nothing, but – the icefall doctor, I was in Lukla once and we stayed in the same place for two days, such a nice guy, good experience, but . . .

We reach Gokyo, where the lodge owner, an aunt of a cousin, lets me use the internet for free. The catch is I have to go to the unheated outside room, a maze of satellite phone wiring and solar batteries, where a creaking PC is connected via LAN cable to the router. I can see my breath.

Unread messages, most on the latest in the brawl circus. So-and-so's 'expert' opinion that Sherpas are, as a culture, fundamentally incapable of violence; so-and-so's equally 'expert' opinion that the jig is up, they've always been spoiled brutes. And then that phrase: The Sherpa Mob. I snort with laughter, and make Sherpa Mobster jokes on Twitter until the cold creeps up to my thighs from the concrete floor and my fingers begin to seize.

I go inside the dining room to warm up. Husband-of-aunt-of-cousin has heard something about an argument but no details, *khai*, someone must have done something to set someone off. But did you hear, Mingma, the icefall doctor, was it two daughters or three . . .

The next day my friends and I trudge for what seems to be an eternity up the glacier to Gokyo's fifth lake. It's the best view of Everest, the lodge owners have assured us – better than from Kalapatthar. When it finally comes into view, Cho Oyu looms to our left as we face eastward – and there it is. Barren black rock, a rather bland dented triangle compared to the beautiful, dramatic ridges that surround it.

All of this, for that.

I see my friends off, and make my way back to Namche. I'm in a lodge kitchen, eating popcorn and listening to four men I don't know, one with wind and sunburn scabs so bad along his cheeks that it looks like reptilian scales. They're fresh down from the climbing season and drinking cans of beer. I think of asking them about the fight, but one begins to talk about how a foreign climber – a woman, not his client – came upon a corpse on the mountain and began wailing and crying and wouldn't move. I had to grab her and shake her, he says, I had to yell at her – if you stop you will die, we'll all die right here, that one's gone already, let it go . . .

The conversation moves on. Spring finishes. The summer fog rolls in, and our elderly neighbours move their livestock up to the high pastures. They come back down occasionally, bringing treats of fresh milk or yoghurt or soft young cheese. Without their animals to feed our scraps to, I spend a lot of time reading about composting techniques. I have a month's work with a group of foreign students. A young Sherpa academic is with us for the first part of the journey. We stop for the night at her aunt's lodge. Her aunt rents horse rides to tourists. 'She's saving any money she gets from that for an iPhone,' she tells me, and we laugh. Later, as a moth flutters above the bed, I wonder what Namgyal might have been saving for. An iPhone costs what an iPhone costs, and so does a future for a baby daughter.

The group of students moves on, often the only foreigners on the trails in the summer mists. In one village we invite the women's savings and credit group to talk to them. A member laughs when she tells me how much they save each week. Their group savings really wouldn't go far up here, where inflation rises steeply every year. 'Being in Sherpa culture has become too expensive in Khumbu,' she says.

The students leave. I stay on, then later try to fly out from Lukla and get stuck in the fog for eight days before the plane arrives. In Kathmandu, the monsoon rains cease and summer finishes. I return in the autumn.

*

It is strange, trying to recall the last time you saw someone who lived, with such comforting regularity, at the periphery of your own life. My mind stubbornly insists that on the last day when my father and I were walking down towards Kathmandu for the winter, Au Tshiri called for us to come in for a cup of tea. But I know this may just be a trick of the brain, a composite of every other time he made that same invitation. In my memory, he's spinning a thread of yak wool through a spindle that dangles from his fingers, but again this may just be echoes from every other time I saw him, leaning in a sunny spot somewhere beside his house with the nasturtiums that grow up the front on strings to guide them, calling out to me, 'When did you come? Where is your father?'

I try now to remember when in the last two years he began building the extension on his home, his retirement plan – a tea shop and bakery. But when exactly, spring or summer or autumn, it was that we got that sack of rice as a contribution to the build and my aunt went down to help with something – digging a trench for a cable, perhaps? It eludes me. It seemed for as long as I could remember there had been the chipping of rocks, the digging of foundations, the laying of stone, the smell of fresh cement as I walked past, observing now a window had gone in, a wall was up, the roof . . . until my father and I stopped in on him one time as we passed – from where? The everyday things you don't make note of – and it was finished, neatly painted, and he was inside making a tray of lamps for an offering. I'll make tea, he said; this can wait – no, no, we replied, we'll come back another time.

It is spring again, and this year I am still in Kathmandu. The heat is stifling; I had forgotten what this time of year is like here. And then, on Friday, the news comes in, the body counts, four, no six, no ten . . . I call my father. I'm okay, he says in his measured, understated way, but things here are not good. Four from our Thame Valley, he says, I heard someone from Khumjung, and two from Pangboche. Au Tshiri went as well.

For a moment, I think I have misunderstood.

On Monday the cremations happen. It was a good day, says my father, very clear and none of the wind or rain that can make a cremation difficult. Au Tshiri's sons were both there. The most auspicious spot was on the slope with the waterfall, you know the one. From there we could see the smoke from another cremation happening down-valley in Phurte. I guess another one was happening up-valley too, but not for the one in Yullajhung, they didn't find his body . . .

A cowardly part of me is glad I am here in Kathmandu with only the hum of the neighbour's generator in my ears, not there, not listening to that conversation multiplied many-fold – so-and-so, from such-and-such a village, and so-and-so, from such-and-such a village, and so-and-so, such a nice man, with daughters and sons and wives and fathers, the brother of this one and the cousin of such-and-such, and the details, repeated over and over, that will break your heart – this was his last season, he said, or he had to go to pay off the debts from his brother's operation, or his leg had only just healed from his last climbing accident two years ago, or his mother had a bad premonition and begged him not to go . . .

I picture next year, at gatherings around Khumbu, when the women sit with the women and the men sit with the men, when the children dart about and pull faces at each other from behind their parents' backs, and the cups of tea are poured and served first to the patriarchs, then to the householders, down to the young fathers and husbands. In each line there will be gaps, like missing teeth – that is, if remaining teeth could all shuffle forward, the way that the adolescents, now a little less awkward than last year, will move a little closer to the fire to fill the spaces of the ones that are missing.

# Sarah Bainbridge
## Speak Up Small Red Thing

A murmur is an indistinct, whispered, or confidential complaint, in low mumbling tones; a mutter, a grumble. A heart murmur is a body's rumour. A muffled voice from a locked windowless room. Anything could be going on in there. The risk of shoulder-barging the door weighed against the risk of walking away. We need to know more. Take a glass, hold it to the wall and press your ear against it.

The stethoscope is the universal sign for doctor. Prior to its invention two hundred years ago, a physician would press his ear directly to the patient's chest to listen to their heart. The first stethoscope was a rolled-up tube of paper. It amplified the sound, and it kept the doctor a respectful distance from the patient, or a welcome distance if the patient had fleas or did not wash.

The term auscultation is derived from Latin. It means 'the act of listening'. During the act of listening the doctor and patient face each other, the distance between them equal to the length of stethoscope tubing. The doctor slides the head of the stethoscope under the patient's clothing and places the cool diaphragm on their chest. The doctor looks over the patient's shoulder, at a fixed point in the near to middle distance, as if the heart hovers there in mid-air. They do not speak. The patient breathes as directed.

First published in *Hue & Cry*, no. 8, 2014. The title is a line from the poem 'Weighing Up the Heart' by Jenny Bornholdt.

The way to describe a heart murmur is four-fold.

First – the location on the chest where the murmur is heard. There are four areas, named for each heart valve. Aortic, pulmonary, mitral, tricuspid.

Second – the timing of the murmur in relation to the normal sounds (the *lub* and *dub*) of the heartbeat.

Third – the grade of murmur intensity on a scale from one to six. One for a very faint sound; six can be heard without a stethoscope.

But the fourth way to describe a murmur is its quality and shape. There are many common terms used, such as crescendo, decrescendo, splitting and continuous. But this category is by far the least prescribed, and it seems that when restricted to the sense of sound and given a small amount of licence, there is a drive towards detailed subjective description. Murmurs are thus characterised as soft, innocent, harmonic, musical, seagull, raucous, honking, blowing, rumbling, vibratory, buzzing, thudding, galloping, scratchy, rasping, machine-like and squeaky. There's the rub and hum, the coarse and harsh. There are knocks and plops, thrills and clicks. There are mammary soufflés.

However, a heart murmur, even beautifully described, is not a diagnosis. It's simply the sound of turbulent blood flow. The sound may be harmless currents and eddies – an 'innocent' murmur, an exuberant, expressive heart. But it can be something more sinister. Looking for a murmur can be a matter of ruling things out. Analogies from home repairs are employed. There may be a hole in a wall between chambers (bad plastering). A valve may not open freely (rusty hinges) or close tightly (leaky washer). There may be inflammation between the outer layer of the heart and the sac it sits in (something to do with cladding).

The next step is an echocardiogram – spying through the keyhole.

Ultrasound has been used to detect faults in ship's hulls, to find icebergs and enemy submarines. Bats use it, dolphins use it. To assess a heart murmur an echocardiogram utilises sound to *see* a sound.

The patient lies on their side with their chest bare. A mildly phallic smooth plastic probe with a blob of clear gel on the end is pressed against their skin. The probe transmits sound and then it listens. It forms an image from the echoes; a wedge of fuzzy static on the screen, until the probe is angled so a slice of the heart comes into view.

The heart's muscular walls appear bright and white, the blood a pool of black. There's a moment of acknowledgement when the patient sees their own heart for the first time, a moment of recognition, of reuniting with an old friend. The men, only ever the men, joke that there's the proof they're not heartless. The image shows the chambers pumping, the valves opening and closing. Yes, says the patient, they look like hands clapping or waving. My heart is waving at me. The blood flow is laid over the black and white image. Its colours are directional. Red flow toward the probe, blue flow away. It's got nothing to do with oxygen.

The probe is moved to different areas on the chest, called windows, where the view to the heart is clear, unobstructed by ribs or lung. At some point the patient asks, 'Can you see the murmur?'

It's explained that the patient cannot have the results right now. The cardiologist will review the scan and write the report. They're not keen on technicians diagnosing their patients. All those years at medical school.

Most often the report reads, 'Structurally normal heart.

No source of murmur demonstrated.' It's a good outcome. The patient is reassured.

But there's something unnerving about finding nothing when a murmur remains. It's not a subjective symptom that can be minimised or explained away. It may be indistinct but it is insistent. It seems the perfect manifestation of doubt. There is turbulent blood flow in every heart, so it's hard to point to any one innocuous swirling current with certainty that it is the murmur's source. All we can say is that we are 'reasonably certain' the sound is not from pathology. How unknowable we are, how indirectly we observe our inner architecture.

## Elizabeth Knox
# Margaret Mahy, Hero

I first met Margaret Mahy when I was working in the shop in the old National Museum, Buckle Street. I met her in *The Haunting*, then, the very next day, in *The Changeover*. I was too old to have read Margaret's picture books as a child, and I sometimes think what it would have been like to have gone on missing her until I had Jack, to whom I read *A Lion in the Meadow*, and *The Boy who was Followed Home*, and *The Great White Man-eating Shark*. As it was, when I was twenty-five I took up reading young adult literature again (after giving it up at fourteen as being something I should grow out of). My renascence began when I picked up Diana Wynne Jones's *A Charmed Life* in a fifty-cent stack in a second-hand bookstore. I plunged back into those books and was reading Wynne Jones and Robert Westall, William Mayne and Antonia Forest and Cynthia Voigt. Then one Saturday morning in the shop I was unpacking book boxes and found a pile of hardbacks of *The Changeover*. I loved the cover – that dark, sombre-faced girl holding up an old coin, or token. That cover *sang* 'heroine' and 'magic'.

My boss Cheryl said, 'You are probably going to want to read the other one first,' and passed me *The Haunting*. (I still don't know whether she thought that the two stories were related, or whether she just wanted to make sure I started

First published on Elizabeth's blog Knoxon, on her website
(http://www.elizabethknox.com/archives/2012/07/24/margaret-mahy-hero/).

with the book she had already read and enjoyed.) I took *The Haunting* home and read it that night, holding it with very clean hands, peering into its right-angled pages, careful not to crease the spine – all of which meant I could return it to the shop looking untouched. I consumed *The Haunting*, and took *The Changeover* home the following night.

It is difficult to describe the impact of that reading. I loved *The Haunting* and *The Changeover* like I loved Diana Wynne Jones – without yet understanding how lucky I'd been to encounter those two writers so early in my young adult reading. But with Margaret I understood I'd met a writer who was *for* me. She was a New Zealander and, reading those two books, I felt that she was building a room in New Zealand literature where I wanted to go, be, hang out, get comfortable. I'd read Maurice Gee and Katherine Mansfield, Patricia Grace and Janet Frame – my big four – and I felt their presence as explorers. They'd gone off in various directions and hammered in their boundary pegs in places that felt less hospitable to me. Margaret's boundary peg was a spar, standing upright in the sand of a sheltered cove, flying the salty remnants of a black flag, and with sea-pink growing around its base.

After that first encounter I read everything I could find, the picture books in stock in our well-stocked shop, and everything in the Wellington Public Library. I bought the YA books as they came out – in hardback – and this was when I was a poor student, so the book buying was quite a commitment. I didn't feel I had to own Wynne Jones; but I had to own Mahy. I can remember my excitement when I found one of her speeches about reading and writing, the first piece of writing by her I'd read that was intended for an adult audience – an audience of librarians and scholars. I remember hitting myself on the head a few times with the literary magazine it appeared in, and then hiding my eyes in the open book. It was Margaret's *thinking* that I wanted to be able to beat into myself, or isolate myself with. Her thinking – always unusual, and always right. How did she do it? How could she always seem to take a different tack and still always head in the right direction? (By this time I was beginning to see that, at least for me, Margaret's boundary marker was in two pieces, and in numerous places. Part of it was buried in the sand in that friendly cove, the other was still attached to a roving vessel, somewhere over the horizon, still flying its black flag, and picking up any treasure it could find.)

So – that was me – working part-time in the museum shop, reading Mahy, and writing my own novel, which was a ghost story, but not a young adult book. Then *After Z-Hour* was published and, lo and behold, Margaret Mahy reviewed it for the *Listener*.

At the time of the publication of my first novel I was both a newly published and a novice writer – still a novice because I wasn't fully literate. I might have been the daughter of an editor, and have attended one or two PEN parties as a young person. I might have seen Witi Ihimaera hiding behind a piano, and a sozzled Denis Glover kissing my sixteen-year-old sister – I'd seen writer antics – but the writing life I imagined was one where I got to talk to other writers about writing. I figured that since Margaret had reviewed my book she'd know I was a *real* writer and it would therefore not be too rude or forward of me to invite her to have a cup of tea with me when I was in Christchurch with my husband at a Booksellers Conference. It was 1988. Margaret came to our hotel at two in the afternoon when Fergus was at a seminar, and we had tea and cakes in my room. She was friendly and nervous. I was a star-struck mess of shyness, enthusiasm and entitlement. She had a cold. At one point she fished in her sleeve for a tissue and pulled out a teabag.

She looked at it. I looked at it. We both laughed and, after that, settled into a conversation about writing – which would have been far more satisfying for her I'm sure if I had written more and really knew something.

Margaret was always very kind, and she had time for people, for readers and teachers, librarians and people running international conferences on this and that. She had time for fellow writers (even youthfully callow fellow writers). She liked to meet people and talk to them, but she did say to me, years later, that when she did 'too much' – being available, pleasing people, being loved, fêted, owned – she'd sometimes feel raw and skinned and would take a long time to settle back into herself, her true self, her born writer's solitary, savage self.

So, there I was, probably providing her with some pleasure and entertainment, but blithely and thoughtlessly taking up her time. It never occurred to me.

Soon after, Cheryl decided that it would be a very fine thing if the museum shop could bring Margaret up for a weekend reading in the theatrette. 'You've met her, you can ask her.' I called Margaret up and asked, and she said yes (as she invariably did). 'And you can stay with us,' I added.

'I'd be delighted to,' she said.

That is how Fergus and I came to be entertaining Margaret – having her all to ourselves – at dinner, at our dilapidated flat. The bed she was offered was sitting on bricks (low beds were in vogue and all my friends were removing their bed legs. Besides – well – bed legs creaked so, and we were all in flats with thin walls . . .). 246 The Terrace, the top back flat, was leaky and draughty, and had torn curtains and a loose weatherboard that went 'thwang, thwang' all night in a northerly.

I feel astonished and rueful looking back on this. But I think how good Margaret was at writing about these things

– the things that young people just don't see, with their sharp senses and vigour and appetite. She could write *for* the young – and gently and coaxingly *against* them too. Her books love their young heroes' capacity, but almost all of those young heroes are, at some point in the story, innocently hardhearted towards their elders.

That night was one of the first of a very few long conversations I had with Margaret. Like most of them, it was shared. (There were others, very rewarding, shared with Kate De Goldi, and Yvonne Mackay's cousin Denise, a Christchurch photographer, and with my infant son Jack and her infant granddaughter Alice on our legs in a café, kept quiet by being fed bits of rosemary roasted potato, but nevertheless gradually covering us with grease till Margaret was looking at me through glasses stippled with tiny fingerprints.)

What was it like to have a conversation with Margaret?

She was widely and deeply read, and curious. But that only describes her habits of acquiring the world, not how her mind worked. Her mind was astonishing (a word she loved). People have remarked on her feeling for myth. But what she had a feeling for was *significance*. She saw possibilities for meaning, for story, in the way ideas fitted together, not mechanically, but as if *this* thought and *that* would suddenly seem subject to the same gravity, as if the way things fell together revealed the star they belonged to – the shining star, or the obscure one, whose only energy is gravity. This meaning-seeing and making was simultaneously playful and serious. It seems to me that her thinking and her work never sought to find a balance between fun and seriousness, fancy and portent. The opposing qualities just partnered up, and wobbled, and danced.

Margaret could say so much, and do so much, with one stroke of the tongue or pen. For instance, I remember yelling

with joy at the line in *The Pirates' Mixed-up Voyage* con-
cerning the philosophical position of the parrot given to
intoning 'Doom and destiny!' With just four or five lines she
produced 1) a very funny joke, and 2) a deeply felt personal
worldview, and 3) a potted history of western philosophy in
all its sober nuttiness. I mean, this was a book for eight- to
eleven-year-olds and it clearly came out of the same mind that
in *The Changeover* spends a certain amount of time – a bit too
long for comfort – contemplating the terror of the death of a
child. Talking to Margaret I always had the sense that there
were things she had made up her mind about for the purposes
of transmitting helpful and thoughtful views to her readers,
and that, *beyond* that, the generative and noticing imagina-
tion that came up with the thoughts was always turning up as
many monsters and paradoxes, and that those monsters and
paradoxes *drove* her as much as her kindness and wisdom and
generosity *led* her.

At some point in that evening in 1988 Fergus and I became
conscious of the wind snoring through the taped-over gaps
in the lounge windows, and the curtains puffing and strut-
ting. What nerds we were, inviting the celebrated writer to
stay because it might be nice for her to have some conversation about books and writing. So we nervously began to tell her
about the flat, which was in this state of dilapidation because
it was part of the long-disputed estate of the madam who had
run most of the brothels in World War II Wellington. 'This was
once a brothel,' we proudly said. The wind got up even more
and the unsecured weatherboard began its thumping. We apol-
ogised again and Margaret said how appropriate it would be to
have a disturbed night in an old brothel because of a loose bawd.

Oh, she would pounce upon a pun! No pun had any hope
of escaping her catlike attention. She'd make a joke, and then

laugh at it herself – and her laugh – croaky, deep, warm, piratical – always urged everyone else to laugh even more.

It's hard to describe what she was like to listen to. What she'd say – you can get the tenor of that by reading the talks and essays in her collection *A Dissolving Ghost*. But the thing was, she could talk like that off the cuff with only a little less structure and polish. I think of the many times I've seen her on stage, in conversation or being interviewed. Her manner always put people at ease, because, whomever she was talking to, she'd treat them the same – or perhaps it was that she'd find exactly the right level to communicate *and* still be the authentic Margaret. However, in those interviews or staged conversations I did sometimes see her interlocutor (great word) ask a question and realise that they were about to receive a peroration rather than an answer. Margaret's talk would go out wide, springing away from the question like a bird leading a predator away from its nest. But she'd always answer the question, and give the answer the question deserved and required. She didn't make points, she made maps. She didn't do soundbites, and following her thinking was often like following the flight of a bird through a forest to find that the bird isn't being birdy – no, the bird is a little god stitching the forest together.

While I've been writing this I've gone to my shelves to find books I need: *The Changeover* and *The Pirates' Mixed-up Voyage* and *The Other Side of Silence* (my favourite book of hers). They are missing. Who has them? *Really, who has them?* And I've been delving into my files to find letters. I found one to a friend describing how 'the best thing about our trip to Christchurch was meeting Margaret Mahy'. 'She came to our hotel room with her daughter Bridget, and Bridget's being there prevented me from too much gushing admiration, because I was worried I might embarrass them both.' And I've found letters from Margaret – letters that are models of Margaretness – so keen and kind.

I'm thinking of her laugh, her hats, her dogs and cats, her winter coughs, her knitted coats, her rainbow wig, and very imposing penguin suit. I'm thinking of her long sentences and pithy quips; of the rose window of the top bedroom or her flat in Cranmer Square; of her empty refrigerator, of her very model of a modern Major General and, in the same vein, her virtuosic 'Bubble Trouble', and the loving rapture in her grandson Harry's eyes when he watched her perform it at the launch of Tessa Duder's Mahy biography.

Charles Dickens was probably Margaret's favourite writer. So I'm also thinking of the beginning of *David Copperfield*: 'Whether I'll turn out to be the hero of my own life, or whether that station will be held by anybody else, these pages must show.' Margaret had absorbed and understood the whimsy and seriousness of that. I am curious to know what she decided about it, if anything, towards the end of her life in regards to herself, especially since so much of her idea of a large and full life was one with a great measure of something self-forgetting – her story-telling and writing.

Here's Margaret, from a 1991 letter, on changeovers. *I expect your house in Aurora Terrace really feels like home now. But houses can be altered so easily. I have just acquired a puppy and it makes me think of the house differently, as a series of dog places and non-dog places, depending on the time of day. Nothing stands still for long, even when it has foundations and four walls.*

# Alice Miller
## Digesting Ourselves

The other night, I turned up for practice with my amateur football team. After a quarter of an hour of running around in the dark, we concluded that no one was going to turn on the field lights, presumably because it was midwinter and any real sports team had shifted their practice inside. So we did what any self-respecting amateurs would do. We went to the pub.

I suppose that all of us around the table at that gentrified new pub with blank white walls – which we forgave because we were wearing shorts and desired pilsner – could have just gone home and Facebooked our thwarted wish to play football, or looked at pictures of our friends playing football in the English morning, or whatever it is that people actually do on Facebook that never seems quite proportionate to the amount of time you spend on it.

Equally, of course, we could have stayed home and read *Paradise Lost* – but that is not what I'm steering towards. What I thought, as I sat and watched the bowls of chips arrive, and the various pints diminish and replenish, was that if we had stayed home to click our way around those blue and white virtual corridors we know so well, we would not have been able to avoid that single square photo which showed up in the corner of our screens. Even if the image isn't of yourself, even if it's a deeply ironic shot of something entirely apart from yourself, or an earnest photo of your own child – that box

Written in 2012 and first published in *Tell You What*, November 2014.

represents *you*. And you're always hovering on the periphery and seemingly directing the action. Yes, in person we have our bodies – we cannot but look out of our own eyes – but sometimes, as the phrase goes, *we forget ourselves*.

But just as Facebook won't ever forget your tiny jpeg, when you're on Facebook that tiny jpeg won't let you forget *you*. You're doubled, watching yourself partake, comment, and even participate in your own exclusion. And no one in those blue and white corridors ever hands you a cold beer.

*

When the railway was raved about in the nineteenth century, Flaubert added it to his top six list of detested things. The railway got people to other places faster, but according to Gustave, it really just allowed them more time to gather together and share in their own stupidity.[*] A few years after Flaubert's musings, Nietzsche wrote:

> Just look at these superfluous people! They are always ill, they vomit their bile and call it a newspaper! They devour one another and cannot even digest themselves.[†]

One might say that Facebook only differs in so far as it is everyone vomiting their bile and calling it Facebook. Nietzsche's thoughts, however, do give new meaning to the word 'feed'.

[*]   Julian Barnes, *Flaubert's Parrot* (London: Jonathan Cape, 1984), p. 108.
[†]   Friedrich Nietzsche, *Thus Spoke Zarathustra: A Book for All and None*, trans.
      R. J. Hollingdale (London: Penguin, 1961), p. 77.

But hating Facebook is too easy, too much like hating news-papers or railways. Perhaps our fear that social media will make us stupider might mean we'll all work harder to see that the slope doesn't get slipperier, or the feeds any faster. We might also remember that in the sixteenth and seventeenth centuries, court poets feared that the introduction of the printing press could devalue their work.*

Besides, there can be something very sweet about Facebook; it acts like the biographer we'll never have – so we're forever laughing and posing and gliding through Paris.

*

'Boredom,' Walter Benjamin famously said, 'is the dream bird that hatches the egg of experience.'

I always had trouble with this quote, and even hoped it was an awkward translation, because I never thought the right word was 'boredom'. I thought boredom was unpleasant. In fact, I had once suggested that boring was the worst thing that anyone could be, and my father had laughed, because his father – a German-Australian devoted member of the Communist Party who married a woman half his age – appar-ently used to say the exact same thing. If I echo him in more than just this sentiment, my future will be, if not necessarily bright, at least not dreary.

But for Benjamin, boredom is not lack of interest and the irritation that all too often accompanies it. He says of the dream bird:

---

* M. H. Abrams and Stephen Greenblatt (eds), *The Norton Anthology of English Literature* (New York: Norton, 2000), vol. 1, p. 488.

His nesting places – the activities that are intimately associated with boredom – are already extinct in the cities and are declining in the country as well. With this the gift for listening is lost and the community of listeners disappears.*

Benjamin's boredom is the self-forgetfulness that accompanied activities like spinning and weaving, that plain space which our brains might occupy now when we're commuting, or taking a long shower. The more we can forget ourselves, the more we are able to listen to others or to the sound of the world.

Today, more than seventy years after Benjamin's essay, if I am forever accompanied by my iPhone, if I am forever downloading emails and tapping out text messages, if I am forever following a trail of internet articles that leap seamlessly from one to another, I may never glance down and notice the cluster of dream birds that happen to be pecking at my ankles.

Whereas when I sit with my football team in the pub listening to a Scotsman talk about oil rigs in the North Sea, I may become more aware of the world beyond me. (Equally, I admit, I might get drunk and talk about myself.) Neuroscience – itself a problematic field, which benefits from our reverence for the word 'science' – suggests that empathy requires neural processes that are slow. We need to step out of the hectic world in order to think of others. We need play. We need boredom.

Walking down the street before Christmas, I am surrounded by tourists, by signs and shop windows advertising possible presents or discounts, and needs I never knew I had which begin

---

*    Walter Benjamin, *Illuminations: Essays and Reflections*, trans. Harry Zohn (New York: Schocken Books, 1969), p. 91.

to blossom from a proclaimed litany of lacks: my teeth are not white enough, my kitchen deprived of stainless steel, my body not yet wrapped in fine, well-cut merino. Once Christmas is over, there should be some reprieve, but no, after Christmas the world is on sale. Banners and lights and voices squeal for my attention, and the crowds become thicker, more desperate. I own a Kindle, which means I can travel with a veritable library which weighs a few ounces, but it also has a shopping trolley icon in the upper left corner. What's in store used to mean what we'd put aside for the future, but now it means what you can buy right now, without even leaving your chair.

\*

I was talking to one of my father's friends after the orchestra one night. Jim is writing a book; he is a retired architect, and has just turned ninety. When he told me he may never finish his book, he explained he simply couldn't work as he used to. He has to sleep so much more. I said this seemed unfair. 'Not unfair,' he corrected. 'Life. We get old.'

We get old. We die. Still our culture keeps offering us 'time-lessness', which is really an embrace of the temporary, a distraction on all fronts, a denial to hide the fact our bodies are failing us, and that we're producing more and more bodies on this planet, a planet we've decided will sustain anything. Along with the past, our sense of the future has degenerated. It is all now.

\*

A few years ago, I was sitting in the crypt at St Paul's in London, reading a slim volume of Orwell essays that had

come with a *London Review of Books* I'd bought to get the
correct bus fare. I'd been poring over the piece about Tolstoy
tearing apart Shakespeare, imagining white-haired Tolstoy as
an intellectual gladiator, taking on long-dead literary giants in
his arena – when a sentence snagged my eye. It said something
to the effect that on balance, life was suffering. As I read this in
the crypt café, two waves inside me crashed against each other.
One said, no, this wasn't true; life, in fact, was, in spite of suffering, beautiful and rewarding – while the other conceded
that of course Orwell had to be right. I dredged up the text
just now, and the exact quote is as follows:

> Most people get a fair amount of fun out of their lives, but on
> balance life is suffering, and only the very young or very foolish
> imagine otherwise.*

I'm sure I felt foolish as I walked out of that crypt, still
arguing with the dead Orwell. I remember I wrote a poem that
mercifully does not survive, asking: even if Orwell was right,
what of the song on the way to the suffering? I was twenty-six.
I knew I didn't know enough about suffering, and I wasn't
sure I wanted to learn.

*

Now we check our devices the way we once looked at our
watches when we were waiting for something to happen, back
when we wore watches, back when we arrived early because
we could not text to say we would be late. Are we merely

---

* George Orwell, *The Collected Essays, Journalism and Letters of George
  Orwell* (Middlesex: Penguin, 1968), vol. 4, p. 344.

distracting ourselves from life's suffering? And if so, is any method of distraction more imperfect than another? Orwell can call me a fool, but I have a proposition. As we digest and regurgitate ourselves, let's remember we still live in a world that doesn't have a shopping trolley icon looming in the left-hand corner, nor an icon enclosing our identity in a jpeg. Let's continue to forage through strange cobbled alleys, and find fountains with statues of long-dead women. To walk so far into the woods that we lose ourselves among the winding possible tracks, the shuffling branches above us, the ground dressed in golden needles. Let's get drunk with our friends, and make our slurred way home to stay up late reading the words of humans from centuries past who can describe what's happening in our own brains. Let's remember that nature may not answer to us, but we'd do well to listen; we'd do well to set off to a wild land we know we'll never reach.

## Chris McDowall
# How to Get Lost

Take an orange from the fruit bowl and stuff it in a bag or pocket, along with a napkin. Open the front door and start walking. Don't look back.

For twenty minutes, walk away from your house. Avoid heading towards a place you know well. Do not start walking to work or a favourite café. If you see someone you recognise, acknowledge them briefly and keep moving. It does not matter which direction you walk in. The important thing is to stride with purpose and give no thought to where you are going. If you feel like running, it is almost certainly the right thing to do.

After opening up a sizable distance between yourself and your home, things will begin to get interesting. Continue walking, but at every junction take the path with which you are least familiar. Soon you will be wandering down streets you never knew existed. Inside each house there are strange people living unfamiliar lives. Politely peek into overgrown gardens, admire aspirational suburban topiaries, notice the patterns mushrooms make as their spores spread and grow between mossy boulders.

Keep walking.

First published on the blog The Space Bar and the Delete Key, a collaboration with Courtney Johnston, April 2012 (https://web.archive.org/web/20130227061420/http://auchonwater.com/2012/04/25/an-exercise-in-getting-lost/).

Soon you will find a place to sit. You'll know it when you see it. There are no perfect places (except for the places that are perfect). Parks are good, but any quiet place with a bench or dry grass will do. Make yourself comfortable, then take out your orange. Siddhartha taught children how to eat tangerines; unknown neighbourhoods teach how to eat oranges.

Bananas are all speed and convenience. Long, sleek, eager-to-please leathery berries. Grip the handle, peel back the protective skin, and absent-mindedly bite off chunks while switching browser tabs. Oranges are the ideal reflective fruit. It's hard to rush an orange. They demand thought and attention. Using a knife or fingers, find your way into the fruit. Focus intently on the orange, or don't focus on it at all (it's all the same). Stash the peel, then turn the flesh over in your hands. When you're ready, gently detach a segment and place it in your mouth. Chew it slowly, consider its sweetness, swallow and then look up.

You are lost. Alone in unfamiliar territory. Untethered but satiated.

There is one important thing left to do.

I leave the discovery of this final step as a task for the reader. Recognising what it is completes the exercise.

## About the Contributors

**Naomi Arnold** grew up in Te Puke and majored in English at the University of Otago, graduating top of her honours class in 2003. She spent four years working and travelling overseas before studying journalism at the University of Canterbury and moving to Nelson, where she was feature writer at the *Nelson Mail* until 2014. Her favourite reporting memories include two months in Antarctica writing science stories and a month in Vancouver covering the fortunes of New Zealand's Winter Olympic team. She now freelances and works on a variety of other projects, some of them with her new neighbour, her mum. She's online at naomiarnold.co.nz.

**Sarah Bainbridge** studied physiology and zoology at Massey University, and has an MA in creative writing from the International Institute of Modern Letters at Victoria University, Wellington. Her writing has appeared in literary journals including *Hue & Cry* and *JAAM*. She was a finalist in the 2012 Royal Society of New Zealand Manhire Prize for Creative Science Writing, and is an echocardiographer by trade.

**José Barbosa** has written for print publications including the now defunct *Real Groove* and *NZ Musician Magazine*. Online his work can be found at pantograph-punch.com, audioculture.co.nz and jfbarbosa.com. He lives in Auckland.

**Steve Braunias** is a staff writer at *Metro* magazine. He also writes the 'Secret Diary' series for the *Sunday Star-Times*, and the 'Housewife Diaries', which is syndicated to six Fairfax newspapers every Saturday. His book *Civilisation* won the 2013 New Zealand Post Award for Best Non-fiction Book of the Year.

**Claire Browning** is a writer and conservation advocate for Forest & Bird. Formerly editor of Brookers' criminal law portfolio, she was co-author of *Adams on Criminal Law* and writer for the *Criminal Reports of New Zealand*. Claire has also written for the blog site Pundit, and in 2012 she published *Beyond Today: A values story about green politics*. Her latest venture at www.wild-life.kiwi is a nature story.

**Greg Bruce** is a freelance writer based in Auckland. His journalism and essays appear regularly in *Metro*, *North & South*, *Sunday* and *New Zealand Geographic*. He has degrees in communication studies and philosophy. He is married and has one daughter.

**Rachel Buchanan** (Taranaki, Te Ātiawa) is the author of *Stop Press: The last days of newspapers* (Scribe, 2013) and *The Parihaka Album: Lest we forget* (Huia, 2009), and the creator of an artist newspaper, *Melbourne Sirius* (2014). Her essays on Taranaki history, ethics and apology have appeared in *Te Pouhere Kōrero* (2012) and the *Australian Humanities Review* (2012).

**Anthony Byrt** is a writer and critic based in Auckland, New Zealand. His writing has appeared in *Artforum International*, *frieze*, the *New Statesman*, *Art World*, *Art New Zealand*, *Landfall* and the *New Zealand Listener*. He has also contributed to several books and exhibition catalogues. He was the 2013 Critical Studies Fellow at Cranbrook Academy of Art, Michigan, and was a finalist in the 2014 Canon Media Awards for his art writing. He is currently working on a book about contemporary New Zealand art.

**Eleanor Catton** was born in Canada in 1985 and raised in New Zealand. Her first novel, *The Rehearsal*, was published in 2008 to critical acclaim, winning several prizes including the UK Society of Authors Betty Trask Award and the Amazon.ca award for Best First Novel. Her second novel, *The Luminaries*, won the 2013 Man Booker Prize. In 2014 she was made a member of the New Zealand Order of Merit. She lives in Auckland, and teaches creative writing at the Manukau Institute of Technology.

**Megan Clayton** is a writer and teacher from Sockburn, Christchurch, where she lives with her husband and two young daughters. Essays and reviews by Megan have been published in *New Zealand Books*, *Metro*, the nzepc, *Takahe*, the *Journal of New Zealand Literature* and the *New Zealand Journal of Adult Learning*. Her poetry has appeared in *4th Floor*, *Enamel* and *Pasture*. Megan maintains the 456 Euthymia blog at 456. harvestbird.com and has a PhD on the poetry of Robin Hyde from the University of Canterbury.

**Paul Ewen's** work has appeared in the British Council's *New Writing* anthology, *Landfall* and *Sport*, and he is a regular contributor to online magazine *Five Dials*. His first novel *Francis Plug: How to be a public author* is published by Galley Beggar Press in the UK.

**David Haywood** is the author of three books. His collection of essays *My First Stabbing* was praised by broadcaster Kim Hill as 'Hugely enjoyable . . . terribly, terribly funny'. David's illustrated satire *Reserve Bank Annual 2010* was described by Steve Braunias as 'comic genius'. His children's book *The Hidden Talent of Albert Otter* has a devoted following in Iceland (no one knows why). In his previous life he obtained a PhD in a particularly obscure area of thermodynamics, and is the listed inventor for patents in wave energy technology and cryocooler systems. When not repairing his quake-damaged house, David writes a blog, Southerly, on Public Address.

**David Herkt** is a writer who lives in Auckland. He has worked as a director / researcher in the television industry and his programmes have won two Qantas / New Zealand Film and Television Awards. He blogs for Public Address, his short stories have been published by *Landfall*, and he reviews for Landfall Review Online and the *Sunday Star-Times* and other Fairfax publications.

**Gregory Kan** is a writer based in Auckland. His first manuscript, a series of poems, was shortlisted for the Kathleen Grattan Poetry Prize in 2013. His work is featured or forthcoming in literary journals such as *brief*, *Hue & Cry*, *otoliths*, *Percutio*, *Sport* and *Turbine*. His most recent series of poems, 'A holding apart of air', features in the catalogue for the exhibition *what is a life?* by the painter Kim Pieters, at the Adam Art Gallery, Wellington.

**Elizabeth Knox** has been a full-time writer since 1997. She has published three autobiographical novellas, ten novels for adults, three novels for teenagers and a collection of essays. Her best known books are *The Vintner's Luck*, and the Dreamhunter Duet (*Dreamhunter* and *Dreamquake*). Her latest are *Mortal Fire* and *Wake*. Elizabeth lives in Wellington with her husband, Fergus Barrowman, her son, Jack, and three cats.

**Nic Low** is a writer and artist of Ngāi Tahu and European descent. Born and raised in Christchurch, he now divides his time between a Melbourne sharehouse and a bush retreat. His first book is *Arms Race*, a collection of mischievous short stories. His second, a literary walking expedition through the Southern Alps, comes out in 2016.

**Tina Makereti** is the author of a novel, *Where the Rēkohu Bone Sings* (Vintage, 2014), and a short story collection, *Once Upon a Time in Aotearoa* (Huia Publishers, 2010), which won the Ngā Kupu Ora Māori Book Awards Fiction Prize 2011. In 2009 she was the recipient of the Royal Society of New Zealand Manhire Prize for Creative Science Writing (non-fiction), and in the same year received the award for Best Short Story Written in English at the Pikihuia Awards for Māori Writers. Tina Makereti teaches creative writing at Massey and Victoria universities. She is of Ngāti Tūwharetoa, Te Ātiawa, Ngāti Maniapoto, Pākehā and Moriori descent.

**Chris McDowall** is a cartographer turned data scientist. Chris typically works with maps, code, animations and graphics, some of which can be seen on fogonwater.com. This is the first time his words have been published in print form.

**Alice Miller** is the author of *The Limits* (Auckland University Press and Shearsman). She holds degrees from the International Institute of Modern Letters and the Iowa Writers' Workshop. Her work has recently appeared in *Boston Review*, *Landfall*, *Narrative*, *Oxford Poetry* and *The American Scholar*. In 2014, Alice was Massey University's Visiting Writer and a Grimshaw Sargeson Fellow. Her website is ackmiller.com.

**Keith Ng** left normal journalism in 2008 because hacks, lobbyists and media-trained automatons overran the prose-space. He writes mostly code these days, but still dabbles in data journalism and experiments with crowdfunding. He hopes that these skills will help him and others rebuild from the ashes of the impending Mediapocalypse. Keith blogs at OnPoint, which can be found on Public Address.

**Jemima Diki Sherpa** is from the Solukumbu area of northeastern Nepal. She studied anthropology and media studies at Victoria University in New Zealand. She works as a freelance writer, editor and community coordinator and writes at whathasgood.com.

**Allan Smith** teaches at Elam School of Fine Arts, Auckland. He has worked as curator at the City Gallery, Wellington; and curator, contemporary art at Auckland Art Gallery. Smith was curator of *Bright Paradise*, the inaugural Auckland Triennial in 2001 at Auckland Art Gallery; and in 2012, of *Running on Pebbles*, for the artist-run space Snakepit. His most recent essay, 'Entropic Steps: rocks, ruin, and increase in John Ruskin, Robert Smithson, and Per Kirkeby', won the best scholarly article prize in the Art Association of Australia and New Zealand journal for 2013. With Layla Tweedie-Cullen, Smith co-edits the speculative art and design publication, *distracted-reader*.

**Lara Strongman** is a writer, curator and art historian based in Christchurch, who writes on culture and society through the lens of contemporary art. She is an award-winning editor: *Parihaka: The Art of Passive Resistance*, which she co-edited with Te Miringa Hohaia and Gregory O'Brien, won the history and biography section of the Montana Book Awards, 2002; while the first survey of New Zealand photography for twenty-five years, *Contemporary New Zealand Photographers*, co-edited with Hannah Holm, won the illustrative category of the Montana Book Awards in 2006. Lara is a regular contributor to art and architecture publications, and reviews TV for Radio New Zealand National.

**Leilani Tamu** is a poet, social commentator, Pacific historian and former New Zealand diplomat. In 2013 she was the Fulbright / Creative New Zealand Writer in Residence at the University of Hawai'i at Mānoa. Prior to this, Leilani worked as a freelance writer with regular contributions appearing in Auckland's *Metro* magazine that tackled issues as diverse as racism, unemployment, property investment, cyber bullying, youth suicide and motherhood. Leilani's work has appeared in a number of publications, including *Mauri Ola*, *Niu Voices*, *Landfall*, *JAAM*, *Griffith Review*, *SPASIFIK* and *Snorkel*. Her first collection of poems, *The Art of Excavation*, was published in August 2014.

**Alice Te Punga Somerville** (Te Ātiawa) is a scholar, poet and irredentist who lives with her husband in Poihākena. She is the author of *Once Were Pacific: Māori connections to Oceania* (University of Minnesota Press, 2012) as well as numerous academic journal articles. She presently teaches indigenous studies at Macquarie University, Sydney, and holds a tenured position as Associate Professor of Pacific Literatures at the University of Hawai'i at Mānoa.

**Giovanni Tiso** is an Italian writer and translator based in Wellington. He writes a regular column on media and memory for the Australian literary journal *Overland* and blogs at Bat, Bean, Beam.

**Simon Wilson** is the editor of *Metro*, a magazine devoted to the culture, current affairs and lifestyle of Auckland city. *Metro* won Best Newsstand Magazine in the 2014 Canon Media Awards, and Simon has won several other awards for his writing on the arts, politics, food and other matters. He has previously worked for *Cuisine*, *Consumer* and the *New Zealand Listener*, and began his career in book publishing as an editor with A. H. & A. W. Reed. In 1994 his novel *The Age of Light* was published by Penguin.

**David Winter** holds a PhD in evolutionary genetics and is a post-doctoral researcher at Arizona State University. He has temporarily left land snails behind to study the effect of mutations in a single-celled creature called *Tetrahymena thermophila*. He writes a blog called The Atavism which is syndicated to Sciblogs, and he doesn't quite understand how anyone can do science without wanting to tell the world about it.

**Ashleigh Young** grew up in Te Kūiti and now lives in Wellington. Her poems and essays have appeared in print and online literary magazines including *Best New Zealand Poems*, *Hue & Cry*, *Sport*, *Turbine*, *Griffith Review* and *Five Dials*. She won the 2009 Landfall Essay Competition and the 2009 Adam Foundation Prize for her manuscript essay collection. Her book of poems, *Magnificent Moon*, was published in 2012 by Victoria University Press. On her blog eyelashroaming.com she writes about memory, mental health and cycling, among other subjects. She works as an editor and co-teaches creative science writing with Rebecca Priestley at Victoria University, Wellington.

## Acknowledgements

'As if there could be true stories,' Jean-Paul Sartre said. 'Things happen in one way, and we retell them in the opposite way.' And as if there could be a finished book in your hands without the work of many fine people. First and foremost, we thank all our contributors for permission to republish their retellings, and we are grateful to *Metro*, *The Pantograph Punch* and *Griffith Review* for permission to reproduce work originally published in those magazines. We also acknowledge the generosity of the editors at other publications in which these pieces first appeared.

We're immensely thankful to the crew at Auckland University Press: Sam Elworthy, who fanned the original spark; Anna Hodge, who expertly shepherded us through the process of turning it into a book; and Katrina Duncan who made it look so beautiful on the page. Thanks to Phillip Kelly for the gorgeous cover, and to the exquisitely sharp-eyed Rebecca Lal for tidying the text. Emily Perkins buoyed us up by being an early and enthusiastic reader of the manuscript. This book was supported by a Quick Response Grant from Creative New Zealand; we're grateful to Jill Rawnsley for her advice and encouragement.

We especially thank all the friends and relations, editors, writers and fellow readers who enthused about the project along the way and pointed us towards more than enough great stories to fill several volumes. Your engagement made this a better book. And we salute all those who make space for great nonfiction to flourish, both on and off the page.

Lastly, to our partners and children for their patience while we read and discussed 'just one more thing' over cups of tea: this one's for you.

We welcome your correspondence at TellYouWhatNZ@gmail.com and on Twitter as @TellYouWhatNZ – join the conversation and tell us what you're reading.